Germany

Bosnia

yprus Iraq Afghanistan

Kenya

E

WESSEX

THE
DEVONSHIRE
AND DORSET
REGIMENT
11th, 39th and 54th of Foot

1958 – 2007

THE
DEVONSHIRE
AND DORSET
REGIMENT

11th, 39th and 54th of Foot

1958 – 2007

Pen & Sword
MILITARY

First published in Great Britain in 2007 by
PEN & SWORD MILITARY
an imprint of
Pen & Sword Books Limited
47 Church Street
Barnsley
S. Yorkshire
S70 2AS

ISBN 978 1 84415 553 8

A CIP catalogue record for this book
is available from the British Library

Printed and bound in England
by CPI

Pen & Sword Books Ltd incorporates the imprints of
Pen & Sword Aviation, Pen & Sword Maritime,
Pen & Sword Military, Wharncliffe Local History, Pen & Sword Select,
Pen & Sword Military Classics and Leo Cooper.

For a complete list of Pen & Sword titles please contact:
PEN & SWORD BOOKS LIMITED
47 Church Street, Barnsley, South Yorkshire, S70 2AS, England.
E-mail: enquiries@pen-and-sword.co.uk
Website: www.pen-and-sword.co.uk

Contents

Introduction

This book does not attempt to be a Regimental History as such – events are too close and the perspective of time is lacking – rather it tries to illustrate the story of The Devonshire and Dorset Regiment using as many high quality images as possible, linked by sufficient text to set both images and events in context. We have tried to cover the full range of the Regimental Family: the 1st Battalion, the Territorial and Volunteer battalions, the Old Comrades, the Cadets, the families and our links to the two Counties through our Freedom towns and Regimental supporters.

Inevitably our coverage cannot be even, although we have tried hard to make it so. During the fifties and sixties, cameras were relatively rare, and colour pictures even more so, whereas today everyone seems to own cameras capable of producing high-quality images. We have examined over 15,000 images and attempted to produce a balanced selection across the years, covering the whole Regimental Family. A major effort has been involved in identifying names; however, in order to be even-handed, we have only used ranks and surnames as it would have been invidious to have used some Christian names, but not others.

The production of this book has taken eighteen months from 'bright idea' to the finished product and it would have been impossible without the support of a great number of people, particularly the editorial team: Derek Thomas, who did the detailed research and produced the first draft of both the manuscript and photographs in just three months; Jeremy Archer, who edited the manuscript, photographs and captions and whose enthusiasm and flair did so much to develop the project; John Mellin, who helped enormously in setting people and places in context, particularly in the early years; Gill Friswell, who started as administrative assistant but who rapidly became indispensable in solving our technical and IT problems; and last, but certainly not least, Don Jellard, whose commitment, drive, energy and sheer hard work kept the project on the road and on schedule, despite what seemed, at times, to be insurmountable problems.

Special thanks must also be given to William 'Bill' Smith, whose vast collection of Regimental photographs forms the basis for much of the earlier part of the book; to John Randle, for his notes and photographs of Cyprus and British Guiana; to Simon Young, who produced the superb artwork which forms the endpapers of the book; to Sue Rouillard of Exeter University, who drew the excellent maps; to Angus 'Tosh' MacIntosh, whose camera work and production knowledge were invaluable; and also to Sylvia Menzies-Earl and Jon Wilkinson at Pen and Sword Books, who could not have been more professional and helpful in turning our ideas and images into the finished product.

Over the last eighteen months, the editorial team has acquired an even deeper respect for the exceptional qualities of the West Country soldier. The Regiment has evolved over forty-eight years from its place in a National Service Army – eighty per cent of whose members had less than two years' service – to its role, both Regular and Volunteer, in the professional British Army of today, whose standards have never been higher. They added lustre to the Regiment's reputation, wherever they served.

Colin Sibun

As Colonel-in-Chief of The Devonshire and Dorset Regiment it gives me great pleasure to contribute a Preface to this splendid account of their distinguished service to the Crown over the past 48 years.

My family has strong links to the Regiment and its predecessors, The Dorset Regiment and the 54th Foot, extending back to Gibraltar in 1802 when the life of my ancestor, Edward, Duke of Kent, the father of Queen Victoria, was saved by the gallant conduct of the 54th. My mother, Princess Marina, Duchess of Kent, was Colonel-in-Chief of The Dorset Regiment and later The Devonshire and Dorset Regiment until her death in 1968 and I was honoured and pleased to succeed her in June 1977.

Over the past 29 years I have visited the battalions of the Regiment many times and have always been struck by the spirit of cheerful professionalism which has been shown by all ranks. I have watched with admiration and pride as the Regiment has forged a reputation second to none on operations in Northern Ireland, Bosnia, Iraq and Afghanistan and I have found that this is a Regiment confident in themselves and in the strength and support of their families, friends and Counties. I am proud to retain my link with The Devonshire and Dorset Regiment as Patron of the Regimental Association and with their successors, The Rifles, as Royal Colonel of the 1st Battalion.

I commend this book to you as a fascinating pictorial account of a West Country regiment still strongly rooted into its Counties and its wider Regimental Family spanning the generations.

HRH The Duke of Kent, KG
Colonel-in-Chief
The Devonshire and Dorset Regiment

Lineage of the
Antecedent Regiments

1685 – The Duke of Beaufort's Musketeers, with precedence established as the 11th Regiment of Foot, raised in Bristol by Colonel Henry Somerset, 1st Duke of Beaufort.

1702 – The 39th Regiment of Foot raised in Ireland by Colonel Richard Coote.

1755 – The 56th Regiment of Foot, renumbered the 54th Regiment of Foot the following year, raised in Salisbury by Lieutenant Colonel John Campbell, later 5th Duke of Argyll.

1782 – Regiments of Foot allied with counties, both as recruiting areas and also as part of their title: 11th (North Devonshire) Regiment of Foot, 39th (East Middlesex) Regiment of Foot and 54th (West Norfolk) Regiment of Foot.

1807 – 39th (East Middlesex) Regiment of Foot is redesignated 39th (Dorsetshire) Regiment of Foot.

1881 – Numerical regimental titles abolished under the reforms of Hugh Childers, Secretary of State for War, following the earlier reforms of Edward Cardwell, one of his predecessors: 11th (North Devonshire) Regiment of Foot becomes The Devonshire Regiment; 39th (Dorsetshire) Regiment of Foot becomes 1st Battalion, The Dorsetshire Regiment while 54th (West Norfolk) Regiment of Foot becomes 2nd Battalion, The Dorsetshire Regiment. Regimental Depôts established at Exeter and Dorchester.

1948 – The Dorsetshire Regiment is renamed The Dorset Regiment.

1958 – The Devonshire Regiment and The Dorset Regiment amalgamate to form The Devonshire and Dorset Regiment.

Affiliated Regiments and Ships
and Bond of Friendship

The Australian Army:
  The Royal New South Wales Regiment
The Canadian Army:
  Les Fusiliers de Sherbrooke
The Malaysian Armed Forces:
  6th Battalion, The Royal Malay Regiment

The Royal Navy:
  HMS *Exeter* (commissioned in 1980)
  HMS *Devonshire* (decommissioned in 1978)

Bond of Friendship:
  Le Deuxième Régiment Etranger d'Infanterie

Chapter 1

Amalgamation

The parade that marked the amalgamation of The Devonshire Regiment with The Dorset Regiment took place at Minden in Germany on 17 May 1958. Those taking part were drawn from the 1st Battalion, The Devonshire Regiment (1 Devon) and the 1st Battalion, The Dorset Regiment (1 Dorset). The parade was commanded by Lieutenant Colonel Guy Young, formerly the Commanding Officer (CO) of 1 Devon, and now the first CO of the newly-formed 1st Battalion, The Devonshire and Dorset Regiment (1 D and D), more commonly referred to in Regimental circles as 'the 1st Battalion'. The amalgamation parade was the culmination of a great deal of hard work by Major General George Wood, Colonel of The Dorset Regiment, and his Devon counterpart, Colonel Monty Westropp.

1 Devon practising for the Amalgamation Parade, Trenchard Barracks, Celle.

The Colonels of the two Regiments had been summoned together to the War Office several months before, to be told by the Chief of the Imperial General Staff, Field Marshal Sir Gerald Templer, that their Regiments were to be amalgamated. General Wood and Colonel Westropp immediately brought their wisdom and experience to bear in ensuring a swift and successful amalgamation between two historic West Country Regiments with a great deal in common. There were already strong links from the service together of 2 Devon and 1 Dorset in 231 (Malta) Brigade during the Second World War. Needless to say, the two Commanding Officers, Lieutenant Colonel Young and Lieutenant Colonel Nicoll of 1 Dorset also played a prominent role in the discussions.

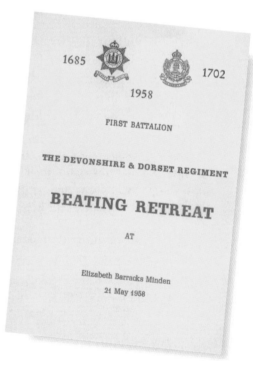

A spontaneous combined Officers' Mess party on the eve of the Amalgamation, Minden, midnight 16 May 1958. Mess songs included: *Widdecombe Fair, The Farmer's Boy, Where Be Yon Blackbird To* and *The Tiddy Oggy Song*: front row (left to right): Robin Sheather, Dickie Turrell, John Hill, Gerald Blight, David Gilchrist, Jim Hewitt, Dickie Thwaytes, John Ives, Roger Woodiwiss; back row (left to right): Bill Tong, John Cann, Bud Wendover, Jeremy Reid, Malcolm Peplow, Peter Baxter, Roger Cullen, Tony Chiswell, Colin Ackford.

These soldiers are relaxing in the NAAFI after the Amalgamation Parade, 17 May 1958: they include (left to right) Cpl Walters, Cpl Gill, L/Cpl Andrews, Cpl Hodge and Cpl Thomas.

The Colours of the 1st Battalion, The Devonshire Regiment and the 1st Battalion, The Dorset Regiment, together with a selection of silver from the Officers' Mess, guarded by Aslt Pnrs wearing No 3 Dress and their traditional aprons. The occasion was an Officers' Mess Regimental Dinner Night at Polemedhia in Cyprus. Only after their return from Cyprus was the 1st Battalion, The Devonshire and Dorset Regiment presented with its first stand of Colours.

Before the parade, details such as cap badges, uniforms, Regimental Colours, Regimental funds, property, affiliations with other regiments and ships and the marking of special historical events had to be decided upon. A base in the counties was of great importance and Topsham Barracks in Exeter was selected as the Regimental Depot. As will be seen, the parade was just the first – albeit the most vital – step. Many of the more sensitive matters were wisely left to evolve over time. Perhaps the two most important of these were Regimental Museums and Regimental Associations. Old Comrades' Associations develop from the camaraderie and demands of their members – and tend to be rather unresponsive to edicts from the War Office! In 1958 allegiances to the former Regiments were naturally extremely strong, stemming as they did from shared experiences in a war that had ended just thirteen years earlier.

With the parade over, Colonel Young naturally wanted to create a cohesive fighting unit as soon as possible. It was therefore particularly helpful that the 1st Battalion left Germany just three months later, staging briefly at Piddlehinton Camp, near Dorchester, before sailing to Cyprus in November, where they would be on operations against EOKA terrorists. Thus there was a real sense of purpose and urgency from the outset. Colonel Young capitalised on this good fortune by taking the Battalion away

The officers of the 1st Battalion, The Devonshire and Dorset Regiment on amalgamation.

		2Lt NJ Wendover	2Lt J Knight	2Lt JR Thwaytes	2Lt JM Hewitt	2Lt RW Cullen	
2Lt D Mitchell	2Lt TDW Slater	2Lt JF Cann	2Lt RD Turrell	2Lt PEG Daubney	2Lt TJB Bryan	2Lt P McL Baxter	2Lt CM Peplow
Lt JCF Hill	Lt CRM Green	Lt AG Chiswell	Lt PM Woodford	Lt CJ Ackford	Lt JW Tong	Lt J Cobb	Lt E Rosenberg	Lt JJ Reid
Capt 'Padre' F White	Lt J Ives	Capt P Burdick	Capt JEK Goodbody	Capt GB Blight	Capt (QM) CV Duffield	Capt R Sheather	Capt RV Woodiwiss	Capt MJ Reynolds	Capt BJ Sims
Capt EC Stones	Maj MFR Bullock	Maj DA Gilchrist	Maj MC Hasting	Col GN Wood	Lt Col GR Young	Col LHM Westropp	Maj C Chettle	Maj JP Randle	Maj SS Elvery	Maj (QM) HAS Titterington

on exercise in the Harz Mountains, from where all ranks marched 100 miles back to Minden. Thus, before even leaving Germany, much had already been achieved. The three-month period at Piddlehinton Camp provided an opportunity for the 1st Battalion to build on this platform and get ready for an operational tour. Everyone had to become familiar with the newly-issued self-loading rifle (SLR) while there were preparations for the disruption that inevitably resulted from a move from one overseas posting to another, but in a very different theatre.

A new brand is launched on the market!

Chapter 2

Cyprus
1958-1961

On 12 November 1958 the 1st Battalion sailed from Southampton for Cyprus aboard the troop transport *Dilwara*. They were seen off by a large crowd of well-wishers and the Regimental Band played a medley of Regimental marches on the quayside. Ten days later, having travelled via Gibraltar and Malta, the *Dilwara* reached Cyprus, where the Battalion, now under a new CO, Lieutenant Colonel Rupert Wheatley, went on operations immediately. The Greek Cypriot community wished for union with Greece, or Enosis, while the Turkish Cypriots wanted partition, or Taksim. EOKA (Ethniki Organosis Kypriakon Agoniston), or The National Organisation of Cypriot Fighters, led by Colonel Grivas, had been trying to force the issue with the British for the previous three years. Three months after the 1st Battalion

British India Steam Navigation Company's MS *Dilwara*, (alias TT *Dilwara*), 12,555 tons.

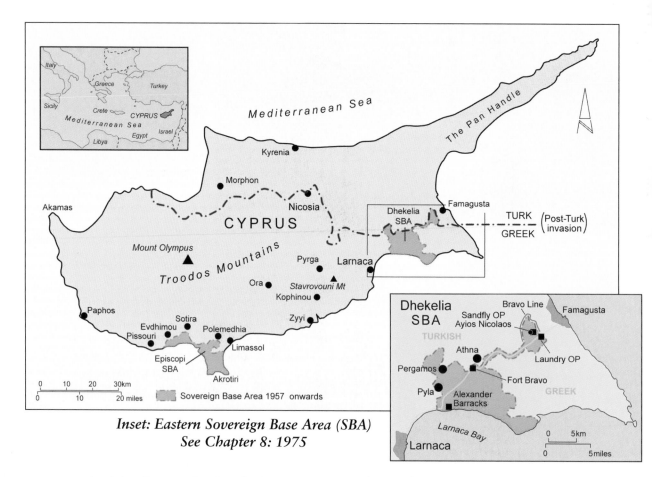

Inset: Eastern Sovereign Base Area (SBA)
See Chapter 8: 1975

arrived in Cyprus the Greek Cypriots' spiritual – and soon to be political – leader Archbishop Makarios returned from a three-year, British-forced exile, first in the Seychelles and later in Athens. Nevertheless, after an upsurge of violence in late summer 1958, Grivas and Makarios were steadily being outmanoeuvred on the political stage. Although the members of the 1st Battalion were scarcely aware of such developments at the time, this phase of the 'troubles' was actually coming to an end. The Battalion's task was to stifle the activities of EOKA within its areas of responsibility and, so far as was possible, to establish a rapport with the local, mainly Greek Cypriot, population.

The 1st Battalion was initially deployed in two quite separate groupings. Battalion Headquarters, B and C Companies went to Waterloo Barracks at Episkopi but were initially required to maintain four of their six platoons at outstations: 7 Platoon was at Phassouri, on the way to Akrotiri; 8 Platoon was at Pissouri Jetty, off the road to Paphos; 9 Platoon was at Evdhimou towards the north while 4 Platoon was at Larnia in the foothills of the Troodos Mountains. B Company's remaining two platoons were held back at Episkopi as the Battalion reserve. The eastern half battalion, comprising A and Support Companies, came under Major Randle and were under command of the Argyll

Newly joined National Servicemen aboard TT *Dilwara:* (left to right) Pte Thomas, Pte Ogborne, Pte Carey, Pte Lidgley, Pte Fitz, Pte Opas and Pte Clements. A ten-day voyage to the Mediterranean sounds exotic but troop transports were extremely cramped and the monotony was only relieved by training and deck sports.

A Coy arrive at Limassol Dock by tender, having disembarked from TT *Dilwara*, November 1958: A Coy and Sp Coy then went east to Kophinou while the remainder of the 1st Battalion went to Episkopi.

Pte Heath and Sgt Hale 'question and search' at a road block on the Ora track.

The base of the MMG Pl, Sp Coy at Pyrga: the dog frequently accompanied patrols.

& Sutherland Highlanders. They were based on Kophinou, at the junction of the Nicosia to Limassol and Larnaca to Limassol roads. That half battalion also deployed platoons to outstations: 1 Platoon to Lefkara; 2 Platoon to Ora and 3 Platoon to Zyyi. The Medium Machine Gun (MMG) Platoon of Support Company was at Pyrga and there was a radio rebroadcast station on Mount Stavrovouni. The reserve, comprising the Mortar and Anti-tank Platoons, was co-located with the two company HQs at Kophinou. Much of their area, too, was within the eastern foothills of the Troodos Mountains and would, under other circumstances, have been most attractive.

Foot and vehicle patrols, road-blocks, café checks, ambushes and searches for the terrorists' favourite culvert bombs became the Battalion's routine, foreshadowing

The base for A Coy and Sp Coy at Kophinou.

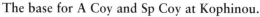

Op *Dettingen* was a two company cordon-and-search of Kornos and nearby villages. This shows two soldiers checking on a culvert. Note the two watching soldiers with mine detector and prodder.

Thunderboxes with a view, Libya 1961: (left to right) Pte Houghton, Pte Copeland and Pte Brooks of the Atk Pl.

Maj Chettle (2IC) and Maj Rouse conduct a vehicle recce.

Troops involved in Op *Dettingen* relax with a brew after an early morning cordon-and-search at Anophritia: (left to right) Lt Burnett, Lt Willes, Capt Reynolds (OC A Coy), Capt Cullen and CSM Allen.

The battalion tug-of-war team including LCpl Rowe, LCpl West, Pte Matterface and their coach, CSgt Taylor.

One of the sections of 7 Pl, C Coy – entirely composed of National Servicemen – at Paxtina Police Station with two Turkish Cypriot policemen.

developments in Northern Ireland little more than ten years later. An early success was a cordon-and-search operation at Sotira and Ayios Therapon, in which 5 and 6 Platoons, under the command of Lieutenant Cobb, approached the objective up an impressive ravine in the midst of a thunderstorm. Weather conditions ensured that surprise was achieved and three wanted men were captured. If only intelligence was always so reliable! A few weeks later B Company assumed responsibility for guarding detention centres at both Pyla and Pergamos, before being redeployed in tented bases on Op *Safari*, essentially undertaking the same role as they had before. Meanwhile C Company caught five so-called 'leafleteers' red-handed and also found nine pistols and eight shotguns. In the eastern operational area, apart from routine patrolling activities, two extensive cordon-and-search operations were mounted, at Kornos and at Kalvasos. A Company's surveillance to the west of Kalvasos led to the arrest of six wanted men while a culvert bomb, believed to have been intended for Major Randle, shook up a forestry official instead.

Matters were progressing swiftly on the political front. The Foreign Ministers of Greece, Turkey and Britain commenced discussions on 18 December 1958 in Paris. The outcome, announced on 19 February 1959, only three months after the 1st Battalion's arrival, was independence for Cyprus but with two permanent Sovereign

20

A *Ferret Mk 2* scout car and *Bedford* 3 ton truck on a resupply mission to one of the outstations: platoons were widely dispersed and vigilance remained essential in order to thwart culvert bombs or terrorist ambushes on roads that were frequently little more than dirt tracks.

As the security situation began to return to normal in the spring of 1959, the first *Sarah Sands* march-and-shoot competition was held: Lt Baxter led the MMG Pl to victory.

The improved security situation gave soldiers the opportunity to explore some of the more scenic parts of the island: Sgt Randle and Cpl Norton on Mount Olympus, Troodos.

Observing the shooting element of the *Sarah Sands* march-and-shoot competition at Pissouri Range: (left to right) WO2 (CSM) Elgie, Capt Reynolds, Lt Col Wheatley, Maj Elvery, Maj Gilchrist (2IC) and Maj Randle. Note the Wyvern cap badge, which was worn at that time by all the regiments of the Wessex Brigade.

All ranks now had a chance to relax without carrying their personal weapons: at a café on the outskirts of Kyrenia (left to right) Pte Lidgley, Pte Reynolds, Pte Harris and Pte Warren.

Soldiers from the 1st Battalion monitored the use of explosives at the iron pyrites mine in the south of the island, as well as guarding the mine itself: these men from 7 Pl were the last to perform those duties.

From mid-1959 there was a return to the normal training cycle: Cpl Cann is preparing this *Mobat* for the next phase of the Atk Cadre at Pyla Range with LCpl Jones and Cpl Walter (both on the right) looking on.

Cpl Walter receiving his Mention in Despatches from Maj Gen Darling, GOC and Director of Operations, with the CO, Lt Col Wheatley, on the right.

Base Areas (SBA) being retained for the British Services, one at Episkopi/Akrotiri and the other at Dhekelia. These arrangements came into effect eighteen months later. The changed situation led to a gradual relaxation of tension, and the withdrawal of British forces from the countryside. By May 1959 the 1st Battalion was reunited at Polemedhia, just north of Limassol, before moving into Kitchener Lines, also at Polemedhia, in August. While these moves were taking place, the demands for guards and other security commitments continued unabated: the MMG and Mortar Platoons had responsibility for the security of the Middle East Broadcast Station at Zyyi, C Company could claim to be the last British garrison at Paphos and A and B Companies took it in turns to guard Government House in Nicosia.

Major General George Wood, the first Colonel of the Regiment, visited the 1st Battalion in early 1959. Another sign of a return to relative normality was the reintroduction of the *Sarah Sands* march-and-shoot competition, won by the MMG Platoon, under Lieutenant Baxter. This was, and remains, an inter-platoon competition to mark the saving of the troopship SS *Sarah Sands* by the officers and men of the 54th Foot, later 2 Dorset, on 11 November 1857. Great care was taken to ensure a balance when adopting the traditions and customs of

The Pakistani 'Charwallah' at Polemedhia Camp: he provided an excellent service with tea and egg banjos on offer at all hours. His son and grandson later followed the family tradition by offering a similar service to soldiers stationed in Northern Ireland. The first tented camp at Polemedhia was fairly basic but the 1st Battalion soon moved into Kitchener Lines, which, though still a tented camp, represented a very considerable improvement.

Cypriot roads and tracks had to be used with care, especially by inexperienced drivers: Pte Turner was fortunate to escape from this *Land Rover* with just a broken arm.

The 1st Battalion Ski Team swept the board at the Near East Ski Championships during the 1960/61 season: (left to right) Capt Reep, Capt Wadham, Lt Hewitt (1st in the Downhill) and 2Lt Wilsey (2nd in the Slalom and in Aggregate). In the early days this was predominantly an officer sport since very few soldiers skied; however, the make-up of the teams shifted later, as will become apparent.

In 1961 A Coy's shooting team took most of the prizes: Cpl Gove (kneeling left), Cpl Williams (kneeling right); seated (front row, left to right) unknown, Sgt Hutchinson, CSM Lamble, Maj Rouse (OC A Coy), 2Lt Thomas and Sgt Barratt. Pte Bennett is behind Maj Rouse's left shoulder.

Cpl Gore leads SSgt Prime, at the Battalion Athletics Meeting, Happy Valley, Episkopi. As one of the few places in Cyprus that were kind to knees, Happy Valley hosted many competitions, including rugby, football and hockey.

the predecessor Regiments. For example, the 1st Battalion first celebrated Wagon Hill Day in Cyprus on 18 January 1960. This commemorates the gallant bayonet charge of

1 Devon during the siege of Ladysmith on 6 January 1900. Three of the five officers who took part were killed and Lieutenant Masterson was wounded and awarded the Victoria Cross. On Wagon Hill Day the Warrant Officers traditionally join the Officers for a formal Guest Night in the Officers' Mess. That May the 1st Battalion celebrated Amalgamation Day with a Trooping of the Colour Parade – which later became known as The Regimental Day. Another sign of reduced tension was the Queen's Birthday Parade, which took place at Limassol on 13 June 1959.

After EOKA finally declared a ceasefire on 24 December 1959, the 1st Battalion at

Sgt Gilbert supervises one of the last live-firing sessions with the *Vickers* Medium Machine Gun: having provided magnificent service over a 50-year span, it was soon to be replaced by the *GPMG (SF)*.

WO2 Shearsby (left) and Sgt Barratt (right) on exercise in Libya: '58 pattern equipment, a '37 pattern pistol holster, studded ammunition boots and … could that be a walking stick?

Trooping the Colour at Polemedhia Camp, Cyprus, 17 May 1961.

last had the opportunity to travel further afield. The first, month-long, Ex *Overlift* took place in Libya the following September – see map on page 34. The exercise covered familiar Second World War locations such as Martuba, Mechili, Derna, Tobruk, El Adem and Cyrenaica. Many of those taking part had the unforgettable experience of visiting the war cemeteries at Knightsbridge and Tobruk. Following the end of Ex *Overlift*, a separate expedition was mounted to Kuffra Oasis. Another aspect of army life was also playing an increasingly prominent role – sport. Both 1 Devon and 1 Dorset had been keen sporting battalions and even between the amalgamation in May and departure for Cyprus six months later, the 1st Battalion achieved third place in the Army Inter-Unit Athletics Championships at Aldershot. The Battalion's football, rugby, hockey, athletics and cross-country teams were particularly strong and the latter swept the board at both Army and Inter-Service levels. To round off a successful season the cross-country team ran a relay round the island, 360 miles in a little over thirty-six hours, in the process shattering the existing RAF-held record. Other popular activities included skiing in the Troodos Mountains and swimming and sailing at Ladies' Mile near Limassol.

Shortly after the return from Libya in October, Lieutenant Colonel Peter Willcocks took over as CO from Lieutenant Colonel Wheatley. At this stage of the new Regiment's life, the COs, most of the Company Commanders and many of the Warrant Officers had earned their spurs in the Second World War. By contrast, the vast majority of junior ranks were two-year, sometimes reluctant, National Servicemen. The turnover was continuous: for example, no less than half the personnel in C Company changed between the autumn exercise in Libya and the next exercise the following March. Another factor was that the strength of each company was far larger than was typical just a couple of years later; B Company had 160 soldiers on strength, of which just sixty were on a regular engagement. This unusual state of affairs presented some real challenges.

A second exercise in Libya took place in March 1961. Once again, the 1st Battalion was flown to the dusty and fly-blown base at Tmimi. This time the Battalion was involved in Brigade Ex *Triangle West* and Ex *Triangle East*, with night attacks and long desert moves becoming a speciality. At the end of these exercises the Battalion sailed back to Cyprus aboard the appropriately-named troop transport *Devonshire*. On return to camp, rehearsals began immediately for the Trooping the Colour Parade on 17 May 1961. This was the last time the Colours of the 1st Battalions of the old Regiments would be 'trooped' since they were to be replaced on the Battalion's return to Plymouth in August 1961. There was one final challenge, Ex *Barbican*, a Brigade exercise held in the foothills of the Troodos Mountains. It was indeed a challenge: exhausting and hot and not likely to be forgotten by those who took part. At 'Endex' even the CO was moved to hoist his shirt on a radio antenna, announcing his 'surrender' to all within earshot!

The 1st Battalion's time in Cyprus was concluded by a fly-past of light aircraft and the playing of 1 Black Watch Pipes and Drums as the 1st Battalion left Famagusta aboard the troop transport *Nevasa*. Some two hundred miles out in the Mediterranean, there was a last tribute from an appreciative Royal Air Force, as two *Canberras* from RAF Akrotiri flew past and dipped their wings in salute.

Chapter 3

Plymouth
1961-1963

The 1st Battalion sailed into Plymouth Sound on 30 August 1961 and moved into an almost-derelict Seaton Barracks and then, shortly afterwards, into Plumer Barracks. The first priority was a spell of leave since many members of the Battalion had been abroad for almost three years. With National Service now being phased out, one of the most important challenges was recruiting. No longer did companies have strengths of 140 to 160. A Company was given North Devon as a recruiting area while C Company went to Dorset. Appropriately-named 'Satisfied Soldiers' visited towns across the two counties while specially selected NCOs were attached to Army Information Offices. Combined Cadet Forces (CCF), Army

LCpl Gale and members of the Recce Pl making an Army recruiting film, autumn 1961: with National Service coming to an end, recruiting had become a top priority.

Under command of 1 RWF, two composite platoons from the 1st Battalion took part in Ex *Pond Jump* in Canada: this platoon was led by Lt Jones and the other by Lt King-Fretts.

Cadet Forces (ACF) and Youth Clubs were given demonstrations and help with training while special displays were mounted at major county occasions such as the Devon County Show. Recruiting was not simply a concern for the 1st Battalion, the problem was Army-wide. Frustratingly, many West Country recruits were siphoned off to battalions higher on the manning priority list. Recruiting would remain an issue until the late 1960s.

There were two high-profile events in late 1961. On 21 October the 1st Battalion provided a Colour Party and Guard of Honour for the laying-up of the Colours of 2 Dorset and 3 Dorset in Sherborne Abbey. Then, on 20 November, the city of Plymouth gave a civic reception in honour of the 1st Battalion. Interspersed with these red-letter days were low-level training commitments at Roborough, Ringmoor, Tregantle and Willsworthy, coupled with basic infantry/tank co-operation at Tidworth, something for which there had been no requirement since leaving Minden.

In March 1962 the 1st Battalion took part in 51 Brigade's Ex *Swan Song*, their first formation level training. Starting on Salisbury Plain, before moving to Stanford, the exercise involved defence and river crossings, as well as the use of helicopters against a nuclear backdrop. Ex *Swan Song* was followed by the 1st Battalion's Rifle Meeting at Tregantle. Spring was devoted to ceremonial events, of which the first was the granting to the Regiment of the Freedom of the City of Exeter on 11 May 1962. After the formal presentation was over, the 1st Battalion marched through the city 'with band playing, bayonets fixed and Colours (the old 1 Devon and 1 Dorset Colours) flying'. This was

The City of Plymouth hosted a magnificent reception soon after the 1st Battalion had returned home from Cyprus: Sgt Riggs – sporting the traditional beard – and the Aslt Pnrs march at the head of the Battalion, autumn 1961.

Part of the recruiting effort: the 1st Battalion's float for the Exeter Carnival, autumn 1961.

On 11 May 1962 the Regiment received the Freedom of Exeter: the Mayor, Alderman Steele-Perkins, presents the Freedom Scroll to the Colonel of the Regiment, Maj Gen Borradaile.

On 26 May 1962 the Colonel-in-Chief, HRH Princess Marina, Duchess of Kent, presented new Colours to the 1st Battalion: the Chaplain General to the Forces, the Venerable Ivor Neil, consecrates the new Colours on Plymouth Hoe.

On 26 May 1962 the old Colours of 1 Devon and 1 Dorset march off for the last time: (left to right) Lt Hill and Lt Hewitt, carrying the 1 Devon Colours, and Lt Andre and Lt Hurst, carrying the 1 Dorset Colours, escorted by Sgt Hill and Sgt Brown.

In the summer of 1962 (left to right) Lt Andre, Cpl Cocks, Lt Bastyan and Cpl Evans, took part in Ex *Arctic II*. Together with Cpl Kaye-Lessor, LCpl Whitlock, Pte Crumpton and Pte Durston, they canoed and trekked in North Norway and Sweden. The post-exercise report suggested that not the least of their problems were the cost of the food and keeping Lt Bastyan away from the Lapp girls.

After twelve years with the Regiment, first with 1 Devon and then with the 1st Battalion, Bandmaster Boulding, who also arranged the Regimental March, left after the Queen's Birthday Parade, Plymouth 1962: Lt Col Willcocks, CO, presents him with a silver cigarette box.

The recruiting effort continues: 3-inch mortars coming into action, firing sand-filled bombs, at the Devon County Show.

followed on 26 May by the presentation of new Colours to the 1st Battalion, the first stand for the new Regiment, by the Colonel-in-Chief, HRH Princess Marina, Duchess of Kent, at a spectacular parade on Plymouth Hoe. Princess Marina had been Colonel-in-Chief of The Dorset Regiment since 1953 and graciously agreed to become the first Colonel-in-Chief of The Devonshire and Dorset Regiment. Her appointment stemmed from the close association that the 54th Foot, and later The Dorset Regiment, had enjoyed with the House of Kent since 1802. On Christmas Eve of that year the 54th Foot had remained staunchly loyal to the Duke of Kent, then Governor of Gibraltar, as drunken soldiers from other regiments broke into their armoury and ran amok in response to the Duke's tightening-up of discipline and closure of some of the town's more disreputable drinking establishments. In gratitude the Duke presented a silver

punchbowl to the 54th Foot, on which is recorded his 'high sense' of the Regiment's 'steady discipline and good conduct'. The Presentation of Colours took place in front of thousands of spectators, including Mr TWH Veale, formerly with 8 Devon, who was awarded the Victoria Cross for rescuing a wounded officer under fire at High Wood on 20 July 1916 during the Battle of the Somme.

By August 1962, with the last National Serviceman gone, a seriously-depleted 1st Battalion was reorganised on a two-company basis, A Company and C Company, just as Lieutenant Colonel John Randle, took over as CO from Lieutenant Colonel Willcocks. The new CO was immediately faced with a demand from Records for a draft of 120 junior NCOs and men to be sent to another battalion of the Wessex

Ex *Massif II* involved a journey by canoe from Le Havre to Marseilles, based on Robert Louis Stephenson's *Voyage of the Cigarette*. The crews comprised Lt King-Fretts and Pte Carre in *Plassey*; Sgt Brown and Pte Penny in *Salamanca*; LCpl Spratt and Pte Cloke in *Dettingen* and LCpl Brooking and Pte Lucy in *Marabout*.

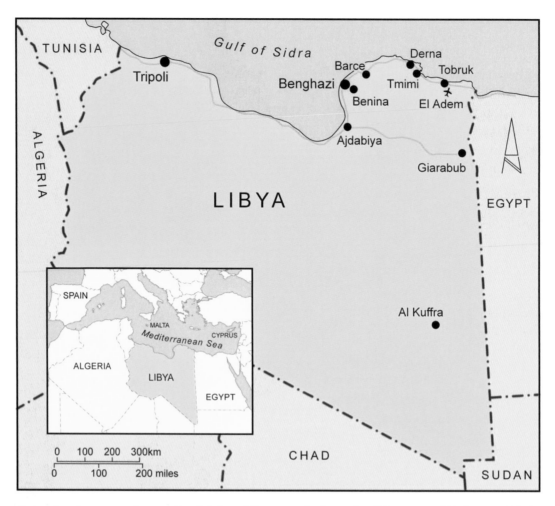

Brigade about to depart for Malta. He appealed to the Director of Infantry, Major General Gleadell, about the state of the Regiment, since such a drastic measure would have reduced the 1st Battalion to less than a company. The appeal succeeded. However, the 1st Battalion was obliged to deploy C Company to Benghazi later in the year. That summer and autumn two platoons participated in Ex *Pond Jump* in Canada while a small expedition went to Norway and Sweden and, during Ex *Massif II*, members of the Battalion canoed across France to the Mediterranean. The Battalion also carried out field-firing at Sennybridge and provided enemy for 51 Brigade's Ex *Cross Belt* on Salisbury Plain.

During the bitterly cold winter of 1962/63, the worst since 1947, the 1st Battalion, now without C Company, was involved in rescuing young soldiers from snow-covered Dartmoor as well as the successful recovery of many sheep and cattle. The latter effort resulted in a special RSPCA award. In January 1963 A Company went to the Cairngorms on winter training, followed by a Battalion deployment to Denmark on Ex *Magic Carpet*, since the Gurkhas had been pulled out of the exercise at short notice. By mid-February Battalion HQ found itself in command of a rifle company of the 1st Battalion with one company apiece of Gurkhas and Danes, operating against two Danish battalions with supporting tanks. While it was a thoroughly enjoyable

Lt Lillies and Pte Cook with *Land Rovers* right down on their springs, heavily-laden with supplies of both petrol and water for a long desert crossing, Libya 1962.

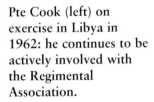

Pte Cook (left) on exercise in Libya in 1962: he continues to be actively involved with the Regimental Association.

Ex *Magic Carpet*, Denmark, February 1963: with Lt Col Randle standing behind him, Col Klokhoj, CO Falsterske Fodregiment, talks to Sgt Riggs, Aslt Pnr Sgt, at Vordingborg Barracks.

The 1st Battalion team won the Army Hockey Cup in 1963: standing (left to right) LCpl Griffiths, Pte Shaddick, Bdsm King, Lt Bastyan, Capt Ackford, Capt Sammons, Sgt Begam, Sgt Wright; sitting (left to right) Capt Hewitt, Sgt Pike, Lt Scrivener, Lt Col Randle (CO), Capt Wadham, Capt Hill.

experience, and much hospitality was offered and gratefully accepted, it clearly demonstrates the manning pressures within the British Army at that time.

It was altogether warmer in Benghazi, where C Company, commanded by Major Hollingshead, enjoyed unaccustomed independence. The early weeks involved range work and field-firing at Derna and acting as enemy to both the Somerset and Cornwall Light Infantry and the Royal Green Jackets on the well-trodden Charruba/El Mechili Track. Suddenly, on 21 February 1963, with key personnel away, the Barce earthquake shattered the calm. For the next five days members of C Company worked desperately hard rescuing those trapped in dangerous buildings, escorting personnel and equipment from Benina airfield to Barce and unloading and distributing urgently required humanitarian stores. C Company was much praised for its efforts, including a personal message from Princess Marina. With the excitement over, they went back to their pre-planned exercises, as well as expeditions into the desert, to Giarabub and the British Petroleum oil rigs.

By April, C Company had returned to Plymouth where, after a much-needed break, they joined the rest of the 1st Battalion on Ex *West End*, an amphibious landing at Carlyon Bay, a helicopter lift to Davidstow and a night attack on Brown Willy, all in torrential rain. Such exercises offer much scope for British humour! A Company then acted as enemy for 130 Brigade's Ex *No Hiding Place* while C Company went on Ex *Colonel Bogey*, a reserve demolition guard on Salisbury Plain. The major sporting triumph of 1963 was winning the Army Hockey Cup: the early promise of the 1st Battalion's hockey team had been carefully nurtured and there were some impressive victories as the team progressed through to the final. After the normal round of farewell parties, the 1st Battalion left for Palace Barracks, Holywood, just outside Belfast, in July 1963.

During the appalling weather of the winter of 1962/63 soldiers of the 1st Battalion rescued large numbers of sheep, horses and cattle on Dartmoor: on 9 December 1963 Lt Col Randle received a Certificate on behalf of the Battalion from Lord Dunleath, representing the Royal Society for the Prevention of Cruelty to Animals.

Chapter 4

Belfast

(including British Guiana 1964)

1963-1965

The Belfast of the mid-1960s was a very different city from the one the British Army came to know so well during the following three decades. The population was welcoming, the atmosphere relaxed and beautiful countryside was on the doorstep to be explored at leisure. Nevertheless there were undercurrents of 'feeling' between Protestants and Catholics while the IRA, though temporarily dormant, was well organised and potentially troublesome. For these reasons, guard duties were more numerous than the 1st Battalion had been accustomed to in Plymouth.

On 13 September 1963 the Band and Drums beat retreat at Holywood Barracks, near Belfast: this was the first occasion on which they wore scarlet tunics and white pith helmets. The difficulties that the similarity of uniform provoked with the Royal Marines were amicably resolved in due course.

An aerial view of Demerara River at Mackenzie, looking south, with Wismar to the right and the Demerara Bauxite Company's plant in the distance, spewing smoke and pollution into the atmosphere.

On balance, however, Palace Barracks and its married quarters were a most welcome improvement on Plumer Barracks and Crownhill Fort. The quarters were close at hand and that proximity, coupled with the 'overseas' nature of Northern Ireland, led to a self-contained 1st Battalion developing a strong *esprit de corps*. The major disadvantage was separation from our recruiting area. Manning remained a challenge, exacerbated as it was by the relatively low priority nature of the role in the Province. To begin with, training took place locally but, later on, two rifle companies re-crossed the Irish Sea and took advantage of an invaluable period of field-firing on Warcop ranges. On their return from Warcop, there was a Beating Retreat at Palace Barracks on 13 September 1963. A new 'tradition' was established that day; the CO, Lieutenant Colonel Randle, had jumped at the offer of some old Devon and old Dorset uniforms from Ordnance and this was to be the first occasion on which the Band and Drums wore scarlet, as they were to do thereafter. The companies were able to spread their wings, to Magilligan for shooting and section and platoon exercises and to Lough Neagh and the River Bann for watermanship. This period culminated in a Brigade test exercise involving a rapid advance on foot and an assault river crossing. A Company won the *Sarah Sands* march-and-shoot, which took place just before Christmas. It was not all work, though: the rugby team had a very successful season while the cross-country team won the Command Championship.

In late January 1964 the 1st Battalion was brought to 7 days' notice to move as a number of trouble-spots threatened to flare up around the world. A month later, as the

The 1st Battalion's notice to move was rapidly reduced from 7 days until the order to move finally came in late May: here C Coy is about to depart for British Guiana, with Lt Thomas on the right of the picture.

The waiting is finally over for a happy Company Commander and his CQMS: Maj Goodbody and CSgt Turney in the aircraft at Aldergrove, Northern Ireland, 23 May 1964.

Within hours of arriving in British Guiana, C Coy was deployed to Mackenzie, where there was serious inter-sectarian rioting, which was soon settled by saturation patrols and several days of curfews. Soldiers return from Wismar: (left to right) Pte Matterface, Pte Waters, Cpl Stapleton and Cpl Cook.

Wismar Police Station was the patrol base on the west side of the river, with Sgt Stannard of Sp Pl, C Coy on the right of the picture: only a very few of the items under the building belonged to members of the 1st Battalion!

situation deteriorated, notice to move was reduced to seventy-two hours. These developments coincided with the annual Administrative Inspection carried out by the Chief of Staff since the Brigade Commander had already left for Aden. As the rest of HQ 39 Brigade prepared to join their commander in Aden, the 1st Battalion was brought to twenty-four hours' notice to move to British Guiana.

British Guiana

For eighteen weeks there had been serious political unrest in British Guiana. Tensions were rising rapidly between those citizens of African descent – enfranchised former slaves – and those citizens of Indian origin, who arrived in the country after the slave trade had come to an end. A state of emergency was declared on 22 May 1964 and C Company arrived at Atkinson Field, about twenty miles south of the capital Georgetown two days later. Temperatures were tropical and the humidity was extremely uncomfortable for the new arrivals. Fortunately an acclimatised working party of the Queen's Own Buffs helped to unload the aircraft, a much-appreciated gesture that set the seal on the close relationship which developed between the two battalions. C Company came under command of 1 Queen's Own Buffs and was immediately warned for deployment to Georgetown. Once again, events would intervene. Meanwhile the main body of the 1st Battalion was left champing at the bit on the other side of the Atlantic!

British Guiana's coastal belt has a high population density, focused on sugar estates and other agricultural industries. For some 200 or 300 miles inland there is just scrub and jungle, before one reaches the Rupununi savannah. Although the coastal belt was blessed with a metalled road and a railway line, further inland there were only a few

A relaxed yet disciplined approach helped defuse a very difficult situation, Mackenzie, June 1964 (left to right): Pte Penny, Cpl Cook, Cpl Spiller and Pte Hutchings.

The early disturbances at Mackenzie had subsided but were about to erupt again as a result of the *Son Chapman* incident: C Coy on patrol on the Wismar/Christianburg side of the Demerara River, June 1964.

Certainly not the style of patrolling that would be acceptable in Northern Ireland or Iraq but it served its purpose in restoring confidence to the local population in British Guiana: Pte Andrews is partly hidden, with Pte Wilson behind him.

On arrival in British Guiana, A Coy deployed to West Coast Demerara and the sugar estates: this patrol, with Pte Woodman facing the camera, is rather surprisingly wearing shorts in the sugar cane and is about to cross a small bridge spanning one of the many monsoon ditches.

Platoon bases were established on the sugar estates, to protect commercial property and were also well separated along the coastal belt: this is the base of 2 Pl, commanded by Lt King-Fretts, at Vergenoegen, West Coast Demerara.

D/Maj Barlow (left) and Pte Hann consider how to tackle one of the more common natural obstacles on British Guiana's roads and tracks.

A Coy deployed to West Coast Demerara: riot damage at Uitflugt.

In due course the companies were rotated and these C Coy men are about to leave Mackenzie by steamer for Atkinson Field and Georgetown: (left to right) Pte Dale, Cpl Spiller, Pte Hutchings (in foreground) and Pte Penny.

dirt tracks, often impassable in the rains. At that time the only access to the interior was along the country's four major rivers: the Essequibo, the Demerara, the Berbice and the Courantyne. Apart from sugar, the major industry was open-cast bauxite mining at Mackenzie, which was Canadian-owned and lay some sixty miles south of Georgetown. The workforce, which was eighty per cent African and twenty per cent Indian, lived mainly in the Christianburg, Wismar and Silvertown districts, west of the Demerara. The better-educated workers, including Europeans from the Demerara Bauxite Company (DEMBA), lived to the east, at Cara Cara and South Mackenzie. Until 25 May unrest had been confined to the coastal belt but that day it erupted at Mackenzie.

At dusk C Company's Support Platoon was flown in and gazed in awe from the air at the glow from numerous houses ablaze west of the river. Their task was to assist the police in restoring order. Patrols were despatched without delay, an immediate and visible presence on the streets being deemed essential. It was reassuring to see the effect that four men with fixed bayonets had on the local population! It was a classic internal security situation, with the 1st Battalion operating 'in aid of the civil power'. The rioters were not anti-British, in the main they were Africans seeking out Indians, burning their property and murdering and raping where opportunities presented themselves. Unfortunately a single platoon, assisted by about thirty African police, was vastly outnumbered by an extremely agitated population of over 10,000. That first night some 1,600 Indian men, women and children sought refuge at the DEMBA Trade School, the platoon's base. Many had received appalling machete wounds and all were traumatised. The headmaster of the Trade School and the platoon's medic, Lance-Corporal Reade RAMC, did a marvellous job in stabilising the situation and treating the wounded.

At 0400 on the 26 May, Major Goodbody reached Mackenzie with 7 Platoon, while 8 Platoon arrived that evening, both extremely welcome reinforcements. Several days of saturation patrols followed; together with a strictly-enforced curfew, they helped to stabilise the situation. During the next few weeks there was a slow return to relative normality. While C Company was engaged in Mackenzie, the rest of the 1st Battalion arrived in British Guiana on 27 and 28 May. A Company, commanded by Major Stone, deployed straight to the sugar estates of West Coast Demerara, while Battalion HQ was established in Georgetown and B Echelon remained at Atkinson Field.

On 6 July 1964 the riverboat *Son Chapman* was blown up several miles downstream from Mackenzie, with the loss of twenty-seven African lives. Unfortunately the news reached Mackenzie before the security forces arrived and elements of the African population went on the rampage on both sides of the river. It took several days of intensive patrolling and rigid curfews for order to be reimposed. Eventually the Indians who had remained in Mackenzie after the May riots were evacuated to the coastal belt

The Drums Pl under 2Lt Steptoe and D/Maj Barlow have come upstream on the River Demerara and are about to come alongside the Mackenzie Stelling, with the wooden buildings of Wismar (left) and Christianberg on the far bank.

After the *Son Chapman* incident, the Police Station at Wismar presents an altogether more operational appearance.

As the security situation improved, adventurous training and 'R and R' trips became possible: the Battalion photographer, Cpl Smith (second from left), enjoys a cup of tea. Over the years his enthusiasm and commitment made a major contribution to the Regiment's photographic archive containing over 20,000 images.

As part of Op *Jungle Bells* platoons hosted Christmas parties for the local children: Pte Martin has been helping to distribute presents at the Amerindian village of St Cuthberts.

Homeward bound, January 1965: the Unit Emplanement Officer (UEO), Capt Cann (back to camera), checks passenger lists at Atkinson Field, with Lt Jefferies, Assistant UEO, on the right.

where, on the sugar estates anyway, the population was predominantly Indian.

As a result of the *Son Chapman* incident, 43 (Lloyds Company) Battery RA, was sent out to reinforce the 1st Battalion in the infantry role since it was feared that the security situation might deteriorate still further. In the event things settled down and the CO was able to rotate the companies, thus giving soldiers the opportunity to go field-firing and adventure training. Places visited included the Rupununi savannah, the spectacular Kaieteur Falls and a battalion leave camp in a fine house on the Essequibo river.

During August and September considerable effort was expended on the recruitment and training of a home guard. The next two months were spent monitoring political meetings before elections on 6 December 1964. The home guard was intended to encourage local people to become involved in their own security. From an organisational point of view the leadership was rather limited, but that did not deter thousands from joining! In the event elections took place without disturbance, which was a tribute to the efforts that the 1st Battalion had put in on the ground.

The last rotation of companies took place in mid-November: A Company took over from C Company on West Coast Berbice and Courantyne, while C Company went to West Coast Demerara. 43 Battery's deployment included a troop at Mackenzie. Following the elections, the Governor, Sir Richard Luyt, asked Forbes Burnham to

2Lt Steptoe makes a new friend in British Guiana!

form a coalition government. The Battalion hosted a series of Christmas and farewell parties, including some for the local children. In a surprisingly short period of time calm was restored to British Guiana. The temperament of the West Country soldier had proved ideally suited to the challenging task. The 1st Battalion left British Guiana in January 1965, reassembling for duty at Palace Barracks in early February, after a spell of block leave. Before the departure from British Guiana the 1st Battalion was fortunate to recruit a dozen well-educated, young Guyanese from ten times that number of applicants.

The Battalion returned from a muggy British Guiana to a chilly British winter and a new set of challenges: yet another Administrative Inspection, a series of training cadres and planning for a new role as a mechanised battalion in the British Army of the Rhine (BAOR) at the end of the year. In the days of the Cold War this was a much higher priority role and the Battalion had to be brought up to strength and new skills acquired to operate as a mechanised battalion in *AFV 432* armoured personnel carriers.

That spring Lieutenant Colonel John Archer took over command of the Battalion from Lieutenant Colonel Randle, who had been awarded the OBE for his leadership during the demanding British Guiana tour. Other awards included an MBE for Major Goodbody, a BEM for Corporal Colley of the Recce Platoon and a Queen's Commendation for Lance-Corporal Reade, who had done so well at Mackenzie. In June A Company went to the West Country on a KAPE (Keeping the Army in the Public Eye) tour while C Company was enemy for 5 Brigade's Ex *Easter Lightning*. The Battalion's farewell to Holywood was a Beating Retreat, this time by floodlight.

Chapter 5

The Wider Regimental Family and TA

1958-1967

The amalgamation of the two regular battalions in May 1958 had been comparatively easy to achieve, driven as it was by a military imperative. Drawing together the more complex threads of the wider Regimental family proved more time-consuming and was necessarily handled with great tact and sensitivity. It had been agreed in 1958 that Regimental Headquarters (RHQ) would be at Topsham (now Wyvern) Barracks at Exeter. Major General Hugh Borradaile, formerly a Devon, acted as Deputy Colonel to Major General Wood, before succeeding

Regimental Cricket week was a popular fixture in the Dorset Regiment calendar and the custom was maintained, Dorchester 1958: sitting (left to right) Lt Hebden, Maj King, Maj Hayes (Captain), Lt Brierley; standing (left to right) Capt Hodge (Secretary), 2Lt Hewitt, Cpl Bulfield, Pte Stubbington, 2Lt Drayton, 2Lt Nickell, 2Lt Hill, 2Lt King, Mr Cripwell (Umpire).

The Dorset Regiment's Reunion and Remembrance Service, Dorchester Cenotaph, September 1958: the Old Comrades of both the Devonshire and Dorset Regiments would maintain parallel Associations for many years to come.

On 8 November 1959 the King's Colour of the 2nd Battalion, The Dorset Regiment (54th Foot) was laid up in Sherborne Abbey: Lt Col White, who commanded 2 Dorset in Burma, represented the Colonel of the Regiment and is seen handing the Colour to Canon Basil Wingfield Digby. Maj Chettle, who won an MC with 2 Dorset at Kohima, is standing behind him. The escorts are Sgt Ellis and WO2 Evans.

In 1958 Devon Army Cadet Force was no less than 1,300 strong and organised into four battalions: here the 4th (Cadet) Battalion are on their Annual Camp at Chickerell.

him as Colonel of the Regiment in 1962, when Brigadier 'Speedy' Bredin, formerly a Dorset, became his Deputy. In 1967 Brigadier Bredin became Colonel of the Regiment and, in this way, the former Regiments took the Colonelcy in their turn. Meanwhile Princess Marina remained Colonel-in-Chief until her death in 1968.

It was decided at the outset that the Old Comrades' Associations of the two former Regiments would retain their independence for the time being and the responsibility for keeping the flag flying in the counties rested with them and with the two Territorial Battalions. Thus it was that the Devon Old Comrades' Association, numbering no less than 670, held a reunion at Exeter, including a memorial service in the Cathedral just two months after amalgamation. The Devons continued to mark such events as the 60th Anniversary of the Relief of Ladysmith in 1960, the laying-up of the old Devon Regiment Colours in 1962 and regular reunions, including one in a marquee at Wyvern Barracks in 1965 during which six Boer War veterans sat together!

It was a similar situation in Dorset, where reunions were centred on Dorchester. Mr W G Hand GC MM was present in 1961, the year that he died. He was one of four Dorset Regiment soldiers awarded Empire Gallantry Medals 'for services rendered in connection with military operations in Malabar, 1921-1922'. This was the largest number ever awarded to a single regiment; they were subsequently exchanged for the newly-instituted George Cross, with which CSM Hand was invested by HM King George VI on 3 February 1942. In October 1961 the Colours of both 2 Dorset and 3 Dorset were laid-up in Sherborne Abbey. Three years later there was another large gathering at Sherborne, including The Dorset Regiment (TA), for the laying-up of the Colours of 1 Dorset.

The Dorset Regiment (TA) were joint winners of the 43 (Wessex) Division Rifle Meeting in 1960: (left to right) Cpl Christopher, Cpl Norman, Sgt Gover, Sgt Cobb, Sgt Nicklen, Cpl Wareham, CSgt Loader, RQMS Felton, Maj Pritchard (Team Captain).

The Devon Regiment (TA) team marched 25 miles a day for four days during the Nijmegen Marches, July 1960: (rear to front) 2Lt Mew, 2Lt Lambert, Sgt Mead (bicycle orderly), Pte Hawke, Lt Harris, Pte Salter, Pte Clancy, Pte Banfield, Pte Stoneman, Maj Dickson, Sgt Alderman, Pte O'Connor, Sgt Rose.

The Devonshire Regiment (1st Rifle Volunteers) TA receiving the Freedom of Exeter on 28 October 1962: the parade was commanded by Lt Col Harrison, with some 200 Old Comrades from 4 Devon, 5 Devon and 6 Devon in attendance.

Under the effective coaching of Maj Turner, Allhallows School CCF won the Ashburton Shield, the premier shooting trophy for schools, in 1960, 1963, 1964 and 1965. This is the winning team from 1960: back row (left to right) Maj Turner, LCpl Montgomery, Cdt Niemann, CSM Hickson; seated (left to right) LCpl Talbot, Cpl Nicholls, Sgt Colby, U/O Crawford, Sgt MacFarlan, Cdt Gilks, Sgt Thatcher; front row (left to right) Cdt Harding, Cdt Jesty, Cdt Parrett.

On 21 October 1961, the Colonel-in-Chief, The Duchess of Kent, attended the laying-up of the Colours of the 2nd and 3rd Battalions, The Dorset Regiment in Sherborne Abbey: she is escorted by the Colonel of the Regiment, Maj Gen Wood, and they are preceded by Yeoman Warder Webber, former RSM of 1 Dorset (nearest camera) and Yeoman Warder Thomas.

The above gatherings illustrate the desire – perhaps even the necessity – for these old soldiers to retain their own links. However, as time went on, it became evident that there was also a pressing requirement for a Devonshire and Dorset Regimental Association, which was duly formed in August 1962. Within just four months there were over 400 members and the first AGM was held at Plumer Barracks in June 1963. Another initiative was the so-called Half-Day's Pay Scheme, whereby every serving man contributed to the Association in order to help those in need. By 1965 membership was approaching the 500 mark and the Devonshire and Dorset Regimental Association was running in parallel with the Old Comrades' Associations of the former Regiments.

The Territorial Army (TA) also played a most important role in fostering Regimental loyalties. At the time of the amalgamation there were two Territorial battalions in the counties: 4 Devon (1st Rifle Volunteers) and 4 Dorset. From November 1959 the battalion numbers were dropped and the two battalions became The Devonshire Regiment (TA) and The Dorset Regiment (TA), which is how the situation remained until 1967. Like the Old Comrades, the Territorial battalions participated fully in county activities, as well as training hard. With the Cold War at its height, the nuclear threat could not be totally discounted and civil defence was one of the key roles. In

On 11 September 1964 the last stand of regular Dorset Regiment Colours were laid up in Sherborne Abbey: here those of 1 Dorset (39th Foot) are marched through a Guard of Honour provided by the Dorset Regiment (TA). The Colour Party was commanded by Capt Robson; the Colour Party Ensigns were 2Lt Tinsley and 2Lt Bull and the Escorts to the Colours were CSM Lambe, CSgt Riglar and CSgt Price.

1958 4 Devon did their civil defence training at Millom while 4 Dorset camped that year at Plasterdown. The following year it was 4 Dorset that went to Millom while 4 Devon participated in amphibious training at Chickerell and Arne. In 1960 the Devonshire Regiment (TA) went to Wretham on Stanford Training Area while the Dorset Regiment (TA) travelled to Barry Budden in Scotland. There was much friendly rivalry between the two battalions and a competitive rifle match took place every year, held either at Sydling St Nicholas in Dorset or at Straight Point, near Exmouth.

As with the 1st Battalion in the early 1960s, the CO, Company Commanders and many of the senior Non-Commissioned Officers (NCOs) had seen active service in the Second World War. As a consequence, many of the exercises had more than a little spice about them. In 1960 Lieutenant Colonel Tony Lewis, who had been a Commando CO in his twenties, took command of The Dorset Regiment (TA). The battalion's exercises the following year were forged from his own experiences: Ex

Members of D Coy, 4 Devon (RV) head for Orcombe Point on Ex *Splash II* in June 1963: members of B Coy, 4 Devon and Devon ACF were also involved.

Breakneck, an amphibious approach and cliff assault at Worbarrow; Ex *Wessex Wade* on Alderney and Ex *Navarone* at Ringstead. Later the Battalion was put through its paces on Ex *Hard Facts* on Salisbury Plain, with a nuclear setting. In 1961 the Devons went to their annual camp at Shorncliffe aboard the destroyer, HMS *Decoy*, and won the China Cup at Bisley. Part-time these battalions may have been, but they were nonetheless extremely proud and professional.

Combined with their training activities, the 'weekend soldiers' also held their heads high within the counties at ceremonial events such as the laying-up of 5 Devon Colours in 1958, the participation of both battalions in the TA Jubilee celebrations in London,

On 25 September 1966 the Devonshire Regiment Old Comrades march to the Cenotaph for their annual service. The previous evening 140 had sat down to dinner at the Victory Club in London "with the sad news of the impending 'death' of our TA Battalions fresh in our minds".

the laying-up of 3 (Militia) Devon Colours in St Andrew's Church, Plymouth, in September 1959, the laying-up of 6 Devon Colours at Barnstaple a week later, the laying-up of 2 Dorset and 3 (Militia) Dorset Colours in Sherborne Abbey in 1961 and the Freedom of Exeter parade in 1962. Both battalions also worked hard to foster links with the junior element of the Regimental family by, for example, including CCF and ACF personnel on some of their exercises, as well as by frequent visits to schools and detachments. They played a key role in maintaining the Regimental presence in the two counties while the 1st Battalion travelled the world.

Within months of being chosen as the Regimental Depot, Topsham Barracks at Exeter was redesignated the Wessex Brigade Depot, serving the five regiments of the Wessex Brigade: The Devonshire and Dorset Regiment, The Gloucestershire Regiment, The Royal Hampshire Regiment, The Wiltshire Regiment and The Royal Berkshire Regiment. It was some consolation that the Depot remained in the West Country and, fortunately, was co-located with RHQ. Wyvern Barracks, as it was then renamed after the Wessex Brigade symbol, was in urgent need of refurbishment and, from August 1961 to April 1964, the Depot moved to the dilapidated Heathfield Camp at Honiton. On its return to Exeter both the Depot and RHQ were well placed to contribute to the Regimental presence and influence within the counties, to support the TA and Cadets and to develop local links. Thus they were able to provide a firm base just as the old TA battalions faced radical change.

A view of the original Main, or Headquarters, Block at Wyvern Barracks, Exeter, showing the splendid Coade stone Royal Arms dating from 1804: a Royal Artillery barracks for many years, Topsham Barracks was renamed Wyvern Barracks in 1964, when it became the Wessex Depot. The mythical 'wyvern', a two-legged dragon, was once the emblem of the Kings of Wessex and it served as the Regimental cap badge until the early 1970s.

Chapter 6

BAOR – Münster and Osnabrück

1965-1969

The next four years of relative stability in BAOR enabled the 1st Battalion to 'mature'. At last the Battalion was given the highest priority for manpower, both the role and associated equipment of a mechanised battalion were demanding while the need to work as an all-arms battle group presented new challenges. After arriving at snow-bound Waterloo Barracks in Münster, built on the site of a *Luftwaffe* wartime airfield, training was soon underway to boost the numbers of drivers, signallers and vehicle commanders. This training gathered momentum as the last batches of armoured personnel carriers (APC), the *AFV 432* series, were delivered. Soon after its arrival Battalion HQ took part in a brigade command post

There was a great deal of training involved as the 1st Battalion prepared for the mechanized role in Germany and re-equipped with the *AFV 432*: Cpl Riggs is the vehicle commander with Pte Beale, his driver, and Cpl Jarrett awaiting his turn.

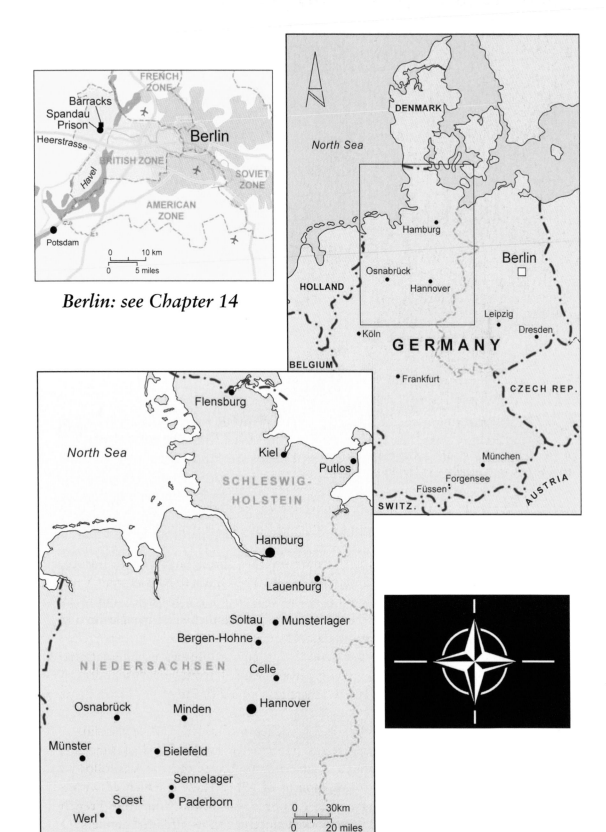

Berlin: see Chapter 14

Cpl Wortley of B Coy supervises night-firing of the platoon level anti-tank weapon, the 84mm *Carl Gustav*, in typically wet training weather.

exercise (CPX) while many of the Battalion were involved in the far larger 1(BR) Corps CPX. There was no better way to gain an understanding of the wider military scene in Germany.

During 1966 many members of the Battalion travelled throughout western Europe. The Band and Drums played at the State Visit of HM The Queen to Brussels and Ypres in mid-May, at a performance of massed bands at Osnabrück and Bielefeld, and at the Queen's Birthday Parade in Münster. Major Lovejoy and some twenty-five Devon and Dorsets took part in a parade at Fontainebleau to say farewell to the French Commander-in-Chief of Allied Forces Central Europe – a prestigious international event – but one that was not without its lighter moments. Despite French withdrawal from direct military involvement in NATO, there was no indication of a reduced threat from the Warsaw Pact.

That summer there was plenty of time for cricket and athletics while the dinghy sailors won the 2 Division Regatta. Others participated in the Handorf Marches, adventurous training at Füssen, sub-aqua diving or golf. A spell of leave was followed by formation exercises during the closing months of 1966. These commenced with a long move with equipment to Larzac, a couple of hours from the French Mediterranean coast. Here the Battalion worked closely with its affiliated gunners, O

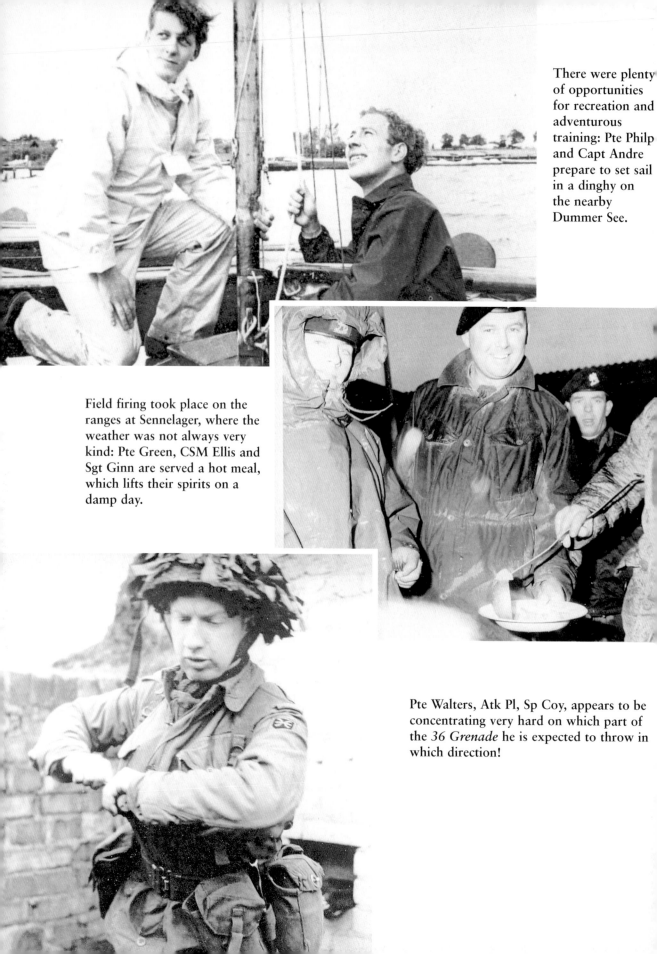

There were plenty of opportunities for recreation and adventurous training: Pte Philp and Capt Andre prepare to set sail in a dinghy on the nearby Dummer See.

Field firing took place on the ranges at Sennelager, where the weather was not always very kind: Pte Green, CSM Ellis and Sgt Ginn are served a hot meal, which lifts their spirits on a damp day.

Pte Walters, Atk Pl, Sp Coy, appears to be concentrating very hard on which part of the *36 Grenade* he is expected to throw in which direction!

A real effort was made at Münster to foster friendly relations with the local German population: D/Maj Barlow leads the Band and Drums through Wolbeck, the Battalion's affiliated village, during the Annual Carnival.

The Colonel-in-Chief, The Duchess of Kent, visited the 1st Battalion on 17 May 1967: she is seen with the Colonel of the Regiment, Brig Bredin, and the CO, Lt Col Archer. At Princess Marina's insistence, she rode in an *AFV 432*, driven by Pte Crumpton, who assured her that he had been cleaning the vehicle for weeks! In addition to the four people already mentioned, the crew also comprised a lady-in-waiting, a private secretary and an ADC, Capt Wilsey.

Pte Harrison helps to pick grapes in the Mosel Valley: such activities offered a welcome change of scene, as well as helping to build relations with the German population.

LCpl Gavican, commander of a *Ferret* scout car, checks his map with great care before giving Cpl Hynes instructions on the next move.

Battery (The Rocket Troop) of 2 Field Regiment, and the armour of C Squadron, 15/19 King's Royal Hussars. Then it was back to the 6 Brigade test exercise at Soltau and Bergen-Hohne where every phase of war, including river crossings, was practised. Finally, there was the 2 Division test exercise. Working as a complete battle group, though not as yet fine-tuned, they crossed the Teutoberger Wald in fog to secure a crossing over the Weser, encountering the Canadian 'enemy' en route. A later phase of the exercise involved recrossing the Weser.

The 6 Brigade Remembrance Day Parade and a successful Annual Administrative Inspection had separated November's exercises. Then there was time for more sport: Battalion teams reached the fourth round of the Army Football Cup and the semi-finals of the Army Hockey Cup. The Battalion also achieved the highest infantry battalion position in alpine skiing. By this time the 1st Battalion was over 700 strong, and was accompanied by more than 800 dependants. Nevertheless personnel turnover was continuous – during 1966, 125 soldiers left while 175 arrived – and the BAOR training cycle was remorseless.

Early the next year there were warm-up CPXs, followed by an experimental, month-long 6 Brigade concentration at Sennelager, covering individual to company-level skills. On 17 May 1967 the Colonel-in-Chief, Princess Marina, visited Münster, accompanied by the new Colonel of the Regiment, Brigadier 'Speedy' Bredin. Within days, the Battalion was flying to El Adem and Tmimi in Libya for Ex *Ballotage*, using pre-positioned APCs. This was a wonderful three-week opportunity for field-firing and manoeuvre on a scale unimaginable in Germany. Unfortunately, with the outbreak of

The 1st Battalion Boxing Team travelled to Ballykinler, Northern Ireland for the Army Boxing Final against 1 Kings. They lost, but only after a plucky performance, with many bearing the marks in this photograph: back row (left to right) Pte Jones, Pte Philbert, LCpl Riley, Pte Thompson, LCpl Smith, LCpl Godfrey, Pte Florence, Capt Hill; front row (left to right) Cpl Murphy, Cpl Wood, Cpl Brown (Captain), SSI Holling, Pte Holden, Pte Hamley, LCpl Sibley. Notable team members missing from this photograph are Bdsm Ballard, LCpl Murphy, Pte Stone, Pte Rodriguez, Pte Penman, Pte Wade and Pte McGarry.

As time in Germany went on, the skiers were able to hone their skills: this is a team from the early days with Capt Wilsey on the left and Cpl Cloke on the right. Other stalwart members of the team included Capt Hewitt, Lt Pook, Lt Hare, LCpl Thomas, Pte Atkinson, LCpl Wilson, Pte McGuire, LCpl Joicey, LCpl Thompson and Cpl Coles.

The soldiers' dining hall at Quebec Barracks, Osnabrück: Cpl Hynes, Cpl Hooton and LCpl Joicey formed an all Recce Pl table.

Osnabrück: LCpl Simon, LCpl Johnston and LCpl Fortune may be discussing travel arrangements over lunch. They were amongst the dozen Guyanese recruited to the Regiment during the 1st Battalion's tour in British Guiana.

Two brothers, Terry and Michael Murphy, working together on an 84mm *Carl Gustav*. The Regiment has always been fortunate in having very strong family links: many brothers served together while sons frequently followed their fathers and nephews followed their uncles.

A typical non-tactical bivouac site on a German training area: Cpl Murphy (left) and Pte Hook (right) relax on a balmy summer's evening.

Pte Adams was responsible for doing the cooking during the 1st Battalion's adventurous training exercises. His main hobby was fishing and, on the basis that his fish were fresher than the issued rations, his activities were initially encouraged ... until the authorities paid a visit! The Police Report included a letter from Füssen District Council in which some serious breaches of the Country Code were revealed: 'Fish from the Schappfensee, cowbells from the meadows and staples of firewood from the forest embezzled were.'

Field training at Larzac in the south of France: Lt Austin allows his patrol, which includes Sgt Gove, Pte Godfrey and Pte Marriott, a brief halt as he checks on the situation.

hostilities between Arabs and Israelis on 5 June, the situation was turned on its head. Disturbances across the Arab world spread to Benghazi, where isolated British military personnel, including families, were living in barracks. According to the Commander Cyrenaica Area: 'Mobs in the town were completely out of control and they attacked and severely damaged both British and American Embassies and, in addition, they wrecked and burnt down the British Council building, the USIS offices, the British Reading Room, our NAAFI Club and a number of Jewish shops. Rioting went on from ten in the morning to eight at night without a stop.' Two hundred miles away across the desert with 'all sub-units dispersed and the second Battle Run in process one company was placed at immediate notice to move to Benghazi in an Internal Security

The medical team at Osnabrück was not only responsible for the serving members of the Battalion, but also for their families: (left to right) Capt Curson, MO, Pte Parsons, LCpl Dally, Pte Heaver and Sgt Barenskie.

Cpl Wright cleans the flotation screen of his *AFV 432* in preparation for one of the frequent equipment inspections: a time-consuming but vital activity. It was always a nervous moment when the flotation screen was put to the test by driving into the River Weser.

Cpl Edgecombe and Pte Reade observe the fire from a *General Purpose Machine Gun* (GPMG), on this occasion being used in the Sustained Fire (SF) role.

There were joint exercises with our NATO allies: Pte McGarry, LCpl Murphy and Pte Bennett (on the extreme right) pose with two Canadian soldiers in front of the latter's very new *M113* armoured personnel carrier.

With Northern Germany criss-crossed by numerous waterways that formed natural obstacles, watermanship was an important part of the Battalion's training. In this photograph, assault boat handling is being practised on the River Weser.

2Lt Delves leads 7 Pl to victory during the *Sarah Sands* march-and-shoot competition in the autumn of 1969.

Ex *Felt 13* was held in Denmark during the summer of 1969 with the Danish Home Guard comprising 'enemy forces': both the Danish 'prisoner' and his captors (left to right) Pte Inch, Pte Titcombe, LCpl Fleming and CSM Simpson of B Company, look very satisfied with the way things have turned out.

role'. Within two hours the whole Battalion was ordered to move to Benghazi: the CO went ahead by helicopter while the rest followed with all speed, avoiding centres of population, but against the flow of Libyan forces heading for Egypt. Sgt Ingram was seriously injured when a Libyan *Saladin* deliberately drove at his *Land Rover*, mounted it on the offside and squashed it almost flat. Having arrived at Benghazi, the 1st Battalion secured D'Aosta and Wavell Barracks while B Company was despatched to El Adem to protect the airfield. The battle group formed two combat teams, Camel and Zebra, with the first acting as a mobile strike force while the second secured Tobruk and activated part of the tank stockpile there. The Battalion also had the unenviable task of moving a vast quantity of stores 80 miles across the desert from Tmimi to the relative security of El Adem. By such actions the 1st Battalion helped to defuse a volatile, and potentially explosive, situation.

A letter from a signaller of 245 Signal Squadron to his father, an ex-Devon, summarises the important contribution made by the Devon and Dorsets: 'Do you know which Battalion came to relieve us? Yes, the Devon and Dorsets. Honestly, Dad, they are the best disciplined and organised battalion I have ever had the luck to serve with. I'm very proud to know that you are an ex-Devon and those lads have certainly not let the name down in any way whatsoever. They are first class in all they do and everybody here is most impressed. Of course, I let them know my father is an ex-Devon. When you go to the next Reunion, you make sure that they know that the young 'uns are as good as ever.'

Back at Münster following Ex *Ballotage* there was a spell of leave, the opportunity for summer sport and grape-picking for some in the Moselle valley. In early autumn Lieutenant Colonel Archer handed over to Lieutenant Colonel Adrian Rouse, just in time for the fast-moving 6 Brigade Ex *Fug Fury*. That was followed by the divisional Ex *Hermelin*. These exercises were challenging – but also great fun – with the 1st Battalion operating at peak efficiency. A week later, as he was conducting the Administrative Inspection, the Brigade Commander spoke to the Warrant Officers and Sergeants in their Mess. Of the Battalion's performance he said: 'Absolutely devastating. You defeated the enemy (and exercise planners) by nine hours on the first day and by twelve hours on the second' – but that was without live ammunition, of course!

By the following year the Army was once again being reduced in size and 6 Brigade was disbanded. Thus the Battalion moved in January 1968 to Osnabrück to join 12 Mechanised Brigade, and into poor accommodation once again, at Quebec Barracks. That winter, the 1st Battalion achieved outstanding success in the boxing ring, winning all

Adventurous training has always formed an important aspect of military life: Capt Jefferies, one of the Regiment's most experienced skippers, at the helm.

After the Soviet invasion of Czechoslovakia, demonstrations within West Germany threatened the security of the Soviet Mission to C-in-C, BAOR (SOXMIS), at Bünde. Two members of the composite Devon and Dorset platoon sent to protect them – Pte Hopkins (left) and Cpl Hann – are pictured with a pair of appreciative Soviet soldiers.

their BAOR matches, before losing to 1 Kings in the Army Boxing Final. Many soldiers were introduced to skiing for the first time during the adventurous training Ex *Snow Queen*, held in the Bavarian Alps. In the spring the training cycle began again, with three weeks of field-firing at Sennelager, followed by a further three weeks of tactical training at Soltau, where the Battalion was joined by C Company of the newly-formed Wessex Volunteers. In June 1968, Major Shortis set up an adventurous training camp at Forgensee in Bavaria. Parties rotated through the camp, taking advantage of the opportunities to canoe, climb and walk in magnificent surroundings. Then it was time to go to Larzac in France once again. B Company exchanged with B Company, 1 Glosters and visited Berlin for two weeks while C Company visited Denmark. At the same time Support Company mounted a KAPE tour to the West Country. Full though BAOR life was, the urgent need for new recruits could never be overlooked: the very survival of the Regiment depended upon its ability to maintain manning levels.

Many members of the Battalion were off station when demonstrations took place throughout West Germany in protest at the Russian invasion of Czechoslovakia on 20 August 1968. The Soviet Mission (SOXMIS) to the Commander-in-Chief, BAOR,

Sgt Newitt, Pte Fowler, Cpl Bienvenue and other adventurous trainers watch Capt Field with rapt attention – and some amusement.

This must be what was amusing them: Capt Field demonstrates the Indian rope trick.

Straddling a knife-edge ridge above Füssen, where the Battalion's Adventurous Training Camp was based.

which was based at nearby Bünde, came under threat and, from a diplomatic point of view, had to be protected. A composite platoon was duly despatched under the MTO, Lieutenant Field. From within the SOXMIS compound they successfully guarded the Soviet Mission and the demonstrations eventually petered out. This was a sensitive task, conducted with speed and efficiency, which elicited grateful thanks from the Russians. Just a week later came the sad news that our Colonel-in-Chief, Princess Marina, had died.

Having hosted the visit by the Joint Services Staff Course in the autumn, the 1st Battalion took part in Ex *Keystone*, the 2 Division work-up, and the last exercise of 1968. Another winter in Germany enabled more soldiers to be introduced to the pleasures of skiing. Both the alpine and langlauf teams met with success, winning the Infantry Cup, although not without mishap, as Lieutenant Hare broke his back. February and March were devoted to the Fitness for Role (FFR) Inspection, which had replaced the old Administrative Inspection. This was followed by individual training at Haltern, which ended with a 40-mile march back to Osnabrück, along the Teutoberger Wald.

Following the amalgamation of two Welsh infantry regiments, the 1st Battalion absorbed around 100 Welshmen, a number of whom swiftly found places in the Battalion rugby team! There was no let-up in the training routine: following the Teutoberger March, B Company (Major Goodbody) formed the infantry element of the 1 (BR) Corps Firepower Demonstration, Ex *Full Blast*; ACF cadets from both Devon and Dorset visited the Battalion for their annual camps while, during the closing months of 1969, the Battalion made a battle procedure film entitled *Castle Key*. There was then a change of command, with Lieutenant Colonel Douglas Lovejoy succeeding Lieutenant Colonel Rouse. There were also feverish preparations for the Battalion's next move. While four years in BAOR had provided both stability and variety, a move to the air-portable role on Malta was certain to provide a complete change.

Chapter 7

Malta GC

(including Belfast 1970)

1970-1971

By January 1970 the 1st Battalion was settled on Malta, in a role far removed from that of their recent experiences in Germany. There was no higher formation, the Battalion had very little technical equipment to worry about and the infantrymen were back to their roots: fitness, skill-at-arms and dismounted, low-level tactics. The first 'real' task fell to the Assault Pioneers, who spent several weeks in Tunisia helping to build a barrier from 400 tons of rock to divert

The 1st Battalion 'A' Team have just won the *Cyprus Walkabout*, April 1970: extremely hot conditions made for a relatively slow time but the important thing was that the RAF were beaten into second place, by 1½ hours: (left to right) Pte McGarry, LCpl Maguire and Capt Thomas. The 1st Battalion 'B' Team – Cpl Cloke, LCpl Fleming and Pte Sidebottom – were third out of a total 55 teams, a fine achievement.

In June 1970 the Battalion went on exercise in Sardinia, acting as enemy and civilian refugees for an assault landing by the US Marine Corps: (left to right) Capt Wilsey, WO2 Cook and Capt Jones, as umpires, watch events unfold, even though not much seems to be happening!

flood water, following serious problems with heavy rains the previous autumn. On 27 April 1970 there was a ceremonial opening of the barrier by the Tunisian Agriculture Minister. Another notable achievement was the success of both 1st Battalion teams in the *Cyprus Walkabout*. Teams had to race sixty miles from Episkopi to the Troodos Mountains, and then back again: the Battalion's teams came first and third, out of a total of fifty-five entries. The Battalion spent the first half of June in southern Sardinia, doing company-level training, after which the Battalion acted as 'enemy forces' as the US 6th Fleet and Marines practised assault landings. The sheer scale of the latter exercise, and the equipment on display, took the breath away. The role was as interesting as it was unorthodox, with soldiers acting as civilian refugees as well as providing armed resistance. On return to Malta everyone was looking forward to a spot of well-deserved relaxation – but it was not to be!

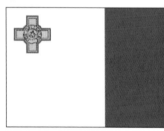

Belfast 1970

In 1969 the Civil Rights Movement had provoked an upsurge in sectarian violence in Ulster and the British Army garrison had been reinforced, to the initial delight of the Catholic community, which welcomed them as their 'protectors'. With the approach of the inflammatory Protestant marching season the following year, the CO was warned that the 1st Battalion should be prepared to reinforce the military presence in the Province in early July. The Chief of the General Staff, General Sir Geoffrey Baker, called Colonel Lovejoy and spoke to him on his bedside telephone, just after the Battalion had been stood down for forty-eight hours. The CGS asked: 'Can your Battalion move tomorrow?' The only possible answer was yes and the British Forces Broadcasting Service put out a call for all Devon and Dorsets to return to barracks immediately. Only one man missed the call. He was in the middle of his wedding when the announcement was made but left the reception and was only two hours late for roll call! Leaving just a small rear party in Malta, 623 officers and men were on the ground in Belfast by 0500

The 1st Battalion deployed to Northern Ireland at very short notice in late June 1970: this was the scene in the King's Hall, Belfast, where the accommodation was extremely cramped.

Still wearing the sand-coloured helmets brought over from Malta, as well as gas masks against the effects of CS gas, the Aslt Pnrs face down a disturbance in the Lower Falls area of Belfast: the 'gentlemen' of the Press were seldom far away.

On a Maltese hillside 2Lt Young and a rather camera-conscious patrol go through the motions for the benefit of Army Public Relations, May 1971: while this may have been an effective recruiting tool, it certainly wouldn't have scored very highly at the tactics wings at either Warminster or Brecon!

Lord Carrington, Secretary of State for Defence, accompanied by Brig Ward, Comd British Troops Malta, is welcomed by Lt Col Lovejoy, CO, and WO2 Tutty on his visit to the 1st Battalion.

LCpl Underwood and Pte Warren practise their FIBUA (Fighting in a Built-up Area) skills, Malta 1970.

When the 1st Battalion was in Malta, the Mortar Concentrations took place in Cyprus: foreground (left to right) Sgt Brown, LCpl Hope, WO2 Tutty and Sgt Harris.

1st Battalion Medical Centre staff, Malta 1970: including, back row (left to right) Pte Johnson, Cpl Fuge, Pte Heaver, Cpl Lewis, Pte Dalley, Pte Pearson; front row (left to right) Cpl Wiltshire, Maj McCallum RAMC, the SSAFA sister and Sgt Barenskie.

The Atk Pl also held their Concentrations on Cyprus, which was a rather less crowded island than Malta: Sgt Farmer considers the situation with Cpl Elms.

Conbats of the Atk Pl in action at Pyla Range, Cyprus: Pte Samuels extracts the spent case while Cpl Westlake observes the effect of the fire.

On 8 April 1971 the 1st Battalion trooped the Colour and held an Open Day: B Coy, Escort to the Colour, present arms.

Members of the Recce Pl on local training in stripped-down *Land Rovers*, Malta 1970: (left to right) LCpl Snow, Pte Reed, Cpl Upton and Sgt Bowden.

on 30 June. It was a remarkable achievement. Commanders were briefed, internal security equipment issued and accommodation allocated in two- and three-tier bunks in the cavernous King's Hall.

On 3 July there was a large find of arms and ammunition in the Lower Falls, a staunchly Catholic area, leading to a well-orchestrated civilian response. Although the platoon from 1 Duke of Edinburgh's Royal Regiment that had made the initial discovery was extracted, albeit with some difficulty, the incident was the catalyst for the so-called 'Battle of the Falls Road'. The 1st Battalion Tactical Headquarters (Tac HQ) and Support Company (Major Bullocke) were soon embroiled in a difficult crowd control situation at the junction of Falls Road with Grosvenor Road and Springfield Road. Support Company advanced into the Falls, linking up with a company of 1 Royal Scots: there were now several thousand troops in the Falls, which was no more than 400 metres square. At one stage Support Company came under sniper attack and returned fire.  They had already used CS gas and baton rounds. Meanwhile B Company (Major Baxter) and C Company (Major Ives) were working with 45 Commando to set up barricades along the Crumlin Road.

When darkness fell, IRA snipers engaged soldiers conveniently illuminated by the street lighting, until harassed soldiers decided to shoot the lights out. Street-by-street the area was cordoned off and the Army, operating in unprecedented numbers,

A beach reconnaissance in calm conditions: (left to right) Sgt Parker, Pte Whatmore and LCpl Scriven.

A Coy helpers at the Gozo orphanage: Mrs Peggy McMaster, WRVS, is second from right on the ground, with Sgt Balston just to the left of centre.

Cpl Loram and Cpl Kendrick managed to find time for sub-aqua, which had a strong following in the Battalion.

Although the 1st Battalion's departure from Malta was delayed, while politicians discussed the future of British Forces on the island, the families had already been sent home. Meanwhile preparations were in hand for the next Northern Ireland emergency tour: 5 Pl, commanded by 2Lt Hamilton, advances at speed to secure a barricade in St. Andrew's Barracks.

imposed a curfew. Detailed searches were conducted in the Falls during the next day: 4 Platoon alone found some 15,000 rounds of ammunition. Within forty-eight hours the Falls was subdued but the 1st Battalion stayed on for a further week, helping to restore order with 1 Green Howards. Later the Battalion was deployed north of the Shankill Road: Dunmore, Snugville and Dunlambert School, where the Colonel of the Regiment visited in August. The Falls operation was a watershed for both Ulster and the British Army and, following it, the security situation deteriorated and the 'Troubles' spread throughout the Province.

After a spell of post-Belfast leave, the Battalion was back at work on Malta by October; however, both B and C Companies managed to spend some time in Cyprus. With Malta still operating as an important naval base, there were opportunities to spend time with the Royal Navy. HMS *Exmouth* took a party to Rome while others had periods at sea aboard HMS *Glamorgan*, HMS *Fife* or HMS *Ark Royal*. The new year ushered in a spell of intense military training with the rifle companies rotating through the Akamas Peninsula on Cyprus and the Support Platoons holding their concentrations on the island. On 8 April 1971 the 1st Battalion trooped the Colour before both the Colonel of the Regiment and the Governor of Malta, Sir Maurice Dorman. That spring the Battalion sent men to Oman on Ex *Great Trek*, a march and navigation competition, while others went on Ex *Cold Nose*, an attachment to the Italian Alpini. The local community was not neglected: A Company (Major Shortis) completed the refurbishment of St Joseph's Orphanage on Gozo, a project begun fifteen months before when platoons from the 1st Battalion had first visited the island. On 30 June a plaque was unveiled in front of a group which included the CO, the Bishop, Major Shortis and Peggy McMaster WRVS, not forgetting the Sisters and a smiling group of children.

Chapter 8

Gillingham

(including Armagh 1972, British Honduras 1972/73, West Belfast 1973/74, Kenya 1974, Cyprus 1975 and Belize 1975)

1971-1976

In late 1971 the 1st Battalion returned from Malta to Gordon Barracks at Gillingham in Kent, remaining in the air-portable role as part of 2 Infantry Brigade. Once again the barracks were in poor condition but, with the 1st Battalion about to embark on an extremely busy programme, that mattered less than it might have done. Training began almost immediately for an operational tour in South Armagh.

Armagh 1972

The 1st Battalion moved into so-called 'Bandit Country' in mid-January 1972: Battalion HQ, A and B Companies (Major Shortis and Major Reid) were based at Gough Barracks in Armagh; Support Company (Major Cobb) was split between Crossmaglen, Forkhill and Newtownhamilton with C Company (Major Jury) starting at Dungannon and Bessbrook, before moving to Newry. A Squadron, Queen's Own Hussars (Major Phipps) was under command at Armagh while Army Air Corps and RAF helicopters were in support.

Initially life revolved around vigorous patrolling, familiarisation with the area and local population, controlling cross-border movement and constant searches. The beautiful landscape had a much darker side. With a view to closing with the population and finding out what was going on, patrolling was usually on foot. Soldiers were most

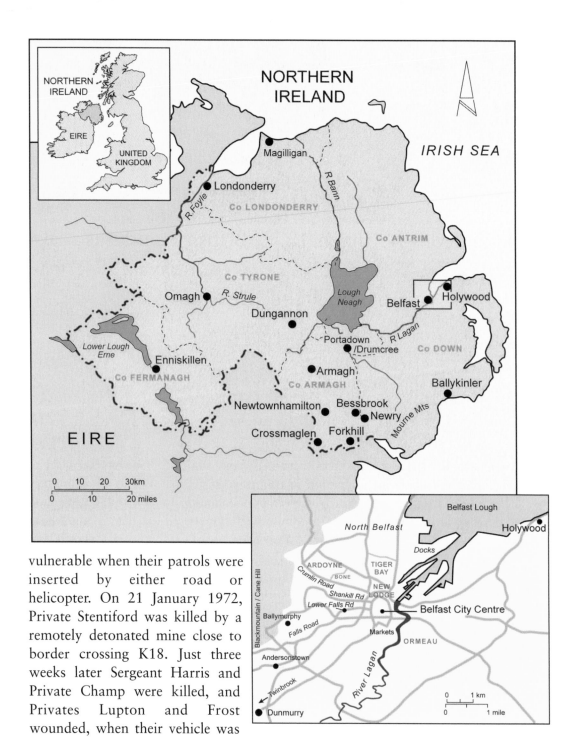

vulnerable when their patrols were inserted by either road or helicopter. On 21 January 1972, Private Stentiford was killed by a remotely detonated mine close to border crossing K18. Just three weeks later Sergeant Harris and Private Champ were killed, and Privates Lupton and Frost wounded, when their vehicle was blown up, also near the border. Effective use of helicopters, called *Eagle Flights*, permitted rapid reaction to incidents and the swift insertion of roadblocks. By such means the terrorists were forced to operate with caution, whether they were moving weapons or people, or setting up culvert bombs.

By mid-March, when Lieutenant Colonel Peter Burdick took over from Lieutenant Colonel Lovejoy, the Battalion had conducted over 1,000 patrols and had found 16lbs

In Northern Ireland beer was limited to just two cans a person a day. This patrol from B Coy has stood down and is relaxing in the canteen: (left to right) Pte Mosley, Cpl Douglas, LCpl John and Cpl Ryan.

The Intelligence Officer offered a bottle of champagne to those who took part in the Battalion's 1,000th patrol: this A Coy group includes Cpl Braund (left) and Pte Janes (second from left).

LCpl Richardson had the narrowest of escapes when his binoculars deflected a round so that it caused no more than a flesh wound: both the binoculars and his jersey (heavy wool) went to the Regimental Museum and he was issued with new kit!

Maj Shortis (OC A Coy), Lt Rogers (OC 2 Pl) and LCpl Riordan after a culvert mine was detonated from over the border during a route clearance operation, Armagh 1972.

Members of 5 Pl, B Coy at Gough Barracks, Armagh, flanked by a *Makralon*-armoured *Land Rover* equipped with loudspeakers and a floodlight on the left and a *Humber* one-ton truck, known affectionately as a 'pig', on the right. This was a special occasion: the cap badges have not been painted black, which had become standard in the 1st Battalion for those on operational tasks.

A briefing takes place before a search operation, Armagh 1972: (left to right) Cpl Peters, Cpl Lewis, Capt Coate, D/Maj Barlow.

The remains of the *Land Rover* in which Sgt Harris and Pte Champ of Sp Coy were travelling near Crossmaglen when a landmine was detonated by remote control under the vehicle – they were both killed in the blast.

of gelignite, 58 feet of fuse, 10 *Claymore* (anti-personnel) boxes, 11 *Claymore* mines, 200lbs of explosives, 32 detonators, an electric pressure switch, three CS gas grenades, three flares, one carbine, two No. 4 rifles, three .22 rifles, four 12-bore shotguns, two .45 revolvers, one .32 revolver, two pistols, one *Sten* gun, one air rifle and 300 rounds of ammunition. During the following month a further 1,000 patrols were carried out. Such intense activity was essential if towns such as Newry were not, effectively, to be surrendered to the Provisional IRA.

On 20 April 1972 a remand prisoner at Armagh Jail seized a police constable's revolver and, with nine other prisoners, took him and two prison officers hostage in the Jail's Reception Centre. Captain Field, the Adjutant, and his team were responsible for the external security of the Jail but now he had to restore order within the Jail itself. Their swift response that day earned Captain Field a Military Cross

> Pte
>
> Since my wife started writing to bloody pen pals we have had nothing but flaming rows.
> I am not saying youre to blame but i would appreciate it if you just dont write again.
> If you do i will take this as a personal insult and you are liable to end up with your teeth kicked in, so to save us both a lot of un-necessary trouble lets just let it go, o.k?

Although the Army officially encouraged 'pen pals', the husbands sometimes got rather upset!

and almost certainly prevented further unrest, both in Armagh Jail and also elsewhere in the Province. Other awards from this challenging tour included Mentions in Dispatches for 2nd Lieutenant Marden and Corporal Bridgeman.

There were happy scenes at Gillingham Station when the 1st Battalion returned from operations in South Armagh: in the event this was to be one of the few occasions in the future that the Battalion returned home by train to be greeted by the Band and relieved families.

Gillingham

Although life back at Gordon Barracks was a little more relaxed, the Recce Platoon's participation in a sleep deprivation trial seemed slightly surprising since that was what they thought that they had been doing for the previous four months! This was also the first opportunity for the 'Welcome to Gillingham' Beating Retreat and Regimental Cocktail Party, which finally took place on 22 June 1972. With the 1st Battalion lower down the manning priority than in BAOR, C Company (Captain Coate) and the Band and Drums was sent on a successful KAPE tour in the West Country. On their return C Company was then pitched into frantic preparations for an activity that could scarcely be more different from the exertions of South Armagh; a month of Public Duties. It was the first time that the Regiment had been so honoured.

British Honduras, 1972-73

The 150-mile border between British Honduras and Guatemala had been disputed by the Guatemalans for many years. It was the British Army's task to secure the border and, to that end, the 1st Battalion, less C and Support Companies, embarked on a six-month unaccompanied tour in British Honduras in August 1972. A combination of extensive jungle training, with  just a chance of operational duties, put a spring in everybody's step. The mission was to 'deter and when the situation demands, defeat an enemy attack on the Colony, or infiltration into it; when so ordered, to provide assistance to the civil authorities in the maintenance of law, order and public morale, with particular reference to the remainder of the hurricane season, and to provide training assistance to the British Honduras Volunteer Guard'. The main base was at Airport Camp where HQ Company (Major Piers) and either A Company (Major Shortis, who was succeeded by Maj Dutton) or B Company (Major Reid) would be based. The second rifle company would be at Holdfast Camp, some 78 miles to the west near the Guatemalan border. Support Company (Major Cann) did not arrive until November, and C Company (Maj Thomas) replaced A Company in January.

The first phase involved extensive reconnaissance, TEWTs (Tactical Exercise

Maj Reid, OC B Coy, briefs some of his Coy at San Ignacio, British Honduras, 1972: while 2Lt King pays great attention to his company commander's familiar gesticulations, Cpl Greenaway and the others look rather confused!

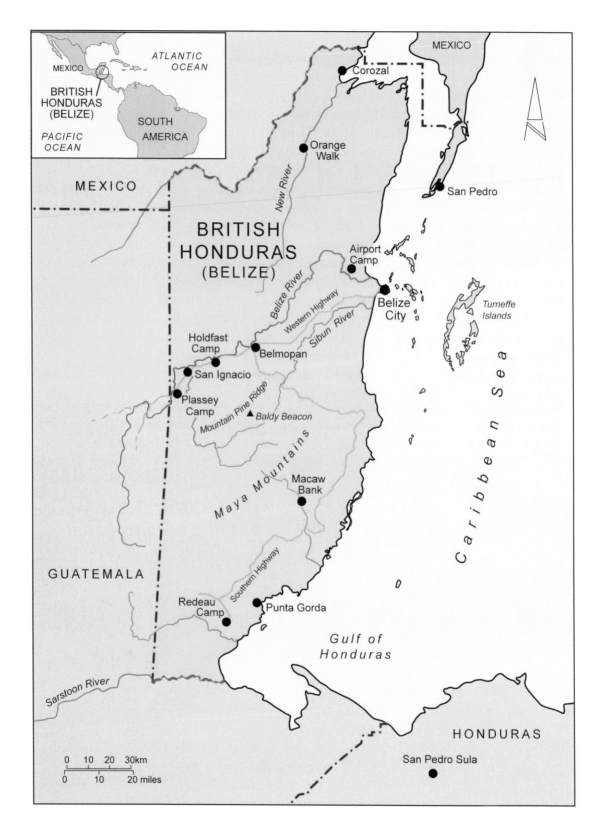

One of A Coy's sections patrol the Belize River – at some speed – in an aluminium assault boat.

Without Troops) and CPXs, and also rehearsals of emergency deployment plans. With initial preparations complete and the threat assessed as low, attention turned to training and other activities. From October it was possible to begin a leave scheme, platoon by platoon, to Merido in Mexico. There was also field-firing at Baldy Beacon: those who took part are unlikely to forget the magnificent view from those bare hills, of the seemingly limitless bowl of dense jungle below, covered by a layer of cloud, before the sun burnt it off.

In October HMS *Plymouth* arrived on station, leading to a series of popular reciprocal visits. Another visitor was an old friend, Donald Mildenhall of the *Western Gazette* and *Pullman's Weekly*, who provided many columns of favourable Regimental coverage in the West Country press over the years. Jungle training involved a great deal of river work, reminiscent of British Guiana: this led to tragedy when Lance-Corporal Phillips of A Company drowned in the Sibun River during jungle warfare training. Sergeant Fallon, also of A Company, received a Commander-in-Chief's Commendation for rescuing Private Bassett from his overturned and burning *Land Rover*.

As part of the British Army's aid to the civil community, each company had its projects: A Company built 'Janner Bridge' near Punta Gorda; assistance was provided by B Company at Corozal, Paraiso and San Pedro, by C

Lord Carrington, Secretary of State for Defence, presents the *Wilkinson Sword of Peace* to the CO, Lt Col Burdick: the award recognised the 1st Battalion's outstanding community work in British Honduras and is still worn today, by the Regimental Sergeant Major of the 1st Battalion when on parade.

While most of the 1st Battalion were serving in British Honduras, C Coy remained behind to carry out Public Duties in London during November and December 1972: the Queen's Guard marches into the forecourt of Buckingham Palace, led by Maj Cullen with 2Lt Hambrook carrying the Queen's Colour.

Company at Orange Walk, by Support Company at Macaw Bank and by the Assault Pioneers at San Ignacio. No less than twenty-five major projects were completed, to the great appreciation of the local community, leading to high praise from the Governor. For these varied endeavours the 1st Battalion was awarded the *Wilkinson Sword of Peace*, which is worn by the Regimental Sergeant Major when on parade.

Gillingham

The bulk of the Battalion rejoined their long-suffering families in Gillingham in February 1973. A Company had come back a month earlier to begin rehearsing for Public Duties, which took place in March and early April. On 5 April the last Captain of the Guard was the Commanding Officer himself. The 1st Battalion was thus well prepared when, on 12 May, the Regiment was granted the Freedoms of the Boroughs of Torbay and Weymouth. The summer was relatively quiet but, back from August leave, it was straight into training for an Op *Banner* tour in West Belfast. Op *Banner* is the official title for military operations in support of the Royal Ulster Constabulary, now the Police Service of Northern Ireland.

West Belfast, 1973-1974

The 1st Battalion deployed into West Belfast on 30 October 1973: Battalion HQ and Support Company were at Fort Monagh; A Company (Major Dutton) and C Company (Major Thomas) were at Woodburn; B Company (Major Piers), with Support Company 1 Welsh Guards (Major Fordham), were based at Glassmullen and Echelon was at Musgrave Park. The areas of responsibility were: A Company – Suffolk, Twinbrook, Dunmurry and Ladybrook; B Company – West Andersonstown; C

Preparing to go out on patrol, West Belfast 1973/74: (left to right) Pte Hughes, Pte Chapman, Cpl Maybry, Pte Martin and LCpl Hann.

LCpl Gilley and Pte Hoskins tune their mine detector during the unsuccessful search for Dr Thomas Niedermayer, a German industrialist and his country's Honorary Consul in Northern Ireland, who had been kidnapped in West Belfast on 27 December 1973 and whose body was not discovered for almost six years.

A particularly cheerful group about to leave on patrol, West Belfast 1973/74: (left to right) Pte Groves, Pte Mosely, Pte Mapp, Pte Simmons, LCpl Keen, LCpl Conway and Cpl Shepherd.

Unknown to Pte Smith, his sister – who was serving in the Women's Royal Army Corps – had also been posted to Belfast: she tracked her brother down and they had an unexpected reunion.

Company – Lenadoon; Support Company – Turf Lodge and Ballymurphy; Support Company 1WG – East Andersonstown. The whole area, previously a two battalion task, was hard Republican and, as a welcome, eighteen shots were fired at Fort Monagh the first evening. During the next four months, IRA-inspired incidents involving shooting, disturbances or other attempts to injure members of the security forces were continuous, but were effectively countered by the professionalism of the officers and men of the 1st Battalion. It seemed that there was an 'incident' most days, of which the following were the most noteworthy: Corporal Murphy of B Company

Members of B Coy, accompanied by Betty on the organ, sing carols at Glassmullen Camp, Christmas Day 1973: (left to right) Pte Jones, Pte Bernard, Pte Davies, Pte Clark and Pte Simpson.

Back in the infantry role after the West Belfast tour: Pte Warren and Pte Taylor with Cpl Toogood of the Recce Pl.

was shot and slightly wounded on 5 November; 8 Platoon found four rifles, a shotgun and a revolver on 6 November; an A Company patrol dispersed an unruly mob on 17 November; on 27 November an alert Recce Platoon OP identified a wounded terrorist, who was duly arrested. Important arrests included those of Ivor Bell, IRA Belfast 'Brigade' Commander, John Daye and Seamus Guinness while, on 27 December, German industrialist Thomas Niedermayer, whose body was not discovered for over six years, was kidnapped from his home in West Belfast. On 2 January 1974 Lieutenant King was slightly wounded when a round grazed his face and, three days later, Lance-Corporal Ali of C Company was severely wounded in both legs.

Fortunately he was evacuated to hospital within minutes. There were major arms finds by Support Company on 23 January and by C Company on 26 January while, on 11 February, Corporal Jellard discovered a booby-trapped garage door.

During the four-month tour, 443 hostile rounds were fired at the members of the 1st Battalion while nine grenades or blast bombs were thrown, or otherwise detonated. Finds included thirty-six firearms, thirty magazines, two telescopic sights, 5,377 rounds of ammunition, one mortar, nine timing devices, twenty-one detonators and 482lbs of explosives. During the tour there were eighteen armed robberies in the Battalion area while 1,225 arrests were made, leading to ninety-three criminal charges. At the end of the tour the Colonel of the Regiment received a fulsome letter of praise from the Commander of 39 Brigade, 'to my mind, their most important achievement was to keep the level of violence down in their area, thus enabling some visible progress towards normality. Rest assured that should they come back to Ireland, I shall be truly delighted to have them back in 39 Brigade'. A few months later the following awards were announced: an OBE for Lieutenant Colonel Burdick, a QGM for Sergeant Riley, Mentions in Despatches for Lieutenant Hambrook and Lieutenant White and the Commander-in-Chief's Commendation for the Chaplain, the Reverend Clayton-Jones.

In July 1974 the bulk of the 1st Battalion went to Kenya on Ex *MacMorris,* which offered excellent opportunities for both field and adventurous training: Bn HQ prepares to move from Archer's Post.

Gillingham

The Battalion returned to Gillingham on 28 February 1974 and immediately went on leave. The pressure on infantry battalions at this time was such that the 1st Battalion had already been warned for the next Northern Ireland tour by the time it went to Kenya on Ex *MacMorris* that July. Money was tight so B Company couldn't go. Battalion HQ was at Nanyuki, in the shadow of Mount Kenya while A, C and Support Companies rotated through Small's Farm, Dol Dol and Archer's Post. These areas, sparsely inhabited but with plenty of wildlife, offered tremendous scope for platoon and company work. The training culminated in an exhausting test exercise at Archer's Post, before everyone relaxed with a few days of adventurous training: climbing Mount Kenya or visiting Lakes Rudolph or Naivasha or the game reserves. B Company's 'treat' that year was a trip to Scotland!

In September 1974, Lieutenant Colonel Colin Shortis took over as CO from Lieutenant Colonel Burdick. It was a sign of the Army's overstretch that, no sooner had the command element returned from their reconnaissance trip to Armagh, the 1st Battalion was warned off for a six-month emergency tour in Cyprus. Time was somehow found for Ex *Peer Gynt*, an inter-platoon competition on Dartmoor, for A and C Companies to perform demonstration duties at RMA Sandhurst and for B and Support Companies to take their turn at Public Duties the following January.

Cyprus, 1975

Just a month later the Battalion flew out to Cyprus. Fearing for the safety of the Turkish Cypriot population – and forestalling a similar move by the Greek Army – Turkey had invaded Cyprus on 20 July 1974, occupying the northern part of the island. Meanwhile British troops were able to secure the Sovereign Base Areas (SBA) and UN Forces monitored the 'Green Line' that

separated the Greek and Turkish communities. The 1st Battalion's task was to 'preserve the integrity of the Eastern SBA (at Dhekelia) against any force and prevent any internal security situation developing' – see map on page 16. The initial deployment was C Company (Major Jefferies) to Ayios Nikolaos, where it protected the important signal monitoring station with its 14-mile perimeter, later wired in by B Company as the 'Bravo Line' when they relieved C Company. B Company (Major Jones) initially manned observation posts, vehicle check points and the observation tower at Athna Village (Fort Bravo), which also protected the Athna Forest Refugee Camp. A Company (Major Coate) began with training and local commitments. The Battalion was based at Alexander Barracks and companies rotated through the various roles.

Once the Battalion had settled into a routine, the relatively calm security situation meant that it was possible to conduct normal training, thus taking advantage of what Cyprus had to offer. Nevertheless there were occasional flare-ups and, in a tragic example on 2 June 1975, Lance-Corporal Dumbleton was killed by a single shotgun

In March 1975 the 1st Battalion replaced a Gurkha battalion on a six-month emergency tour in Cyprus: Pte Guppy, LCpl Bray and Pte Hunt familiarise themselves with their responsibilities at the OP overlooking Pyla Village, one of many potential flashpoints between the Greek and Turkish Cypriot communities.

A group of C Coy officers and SNCOs, Cyprus, summer 1975: standing (left to right) Cpl Butcher, Sgt Crawford, Sgt Jarrett, Sgt Peters, Sgt Wood, Sgt Kelly; seated (left to right) 2Lt Gray, WO2 (CSM) Gallwey, Maj Jefferies, Lt Hambrook, 2Lt Hodgson.

The Bandmaster, WO1 Garrity, conducts a concert by the Band and Drums in Athna Forest: they were entertaining those unfortunates who found themselves in the refugee camp as a result of the Turkish invasion of Northern Cyprus.

Maj Jefferies and C Coy, at that time the 'Champion Company', lead the 1st Battalion from Alexander Barracks to Dhekelia Garrison Church for Church Parade.

Greek Cypriots continued to farm their land adjacent to the Turkish-occupied zone: one of the 1st Battalion's many tasks that summer was to provide protection parties – this one is from 8 Pl – to enable them to do so.

Mrs Sylvia Shortis, the CO's wife, cuts the cake at a children's party: support from the Families' Office and mutual support between families was extremely important when the Battalion was away on operational tours or lengthy exercises.

Comd Coy took the Minor Units Trophy at the Nearelf Skill-at-Arms Meeting: back row (left to right) Sgt Jones, CSM Coker, Capt Shaw, Sgt Tucker, Sgt Bennett, Cpl Ash; front row LCpl Winter, Pte Maple.

Nearelf Skill-at-Arms Meeting: Maj Jones (middle row, third from right) relaxes with members of B Coy after a hard day's work in the butts.

The QM's Pl relax in a Cyprus café: they include (from the left) Sgt Hicks, Cpl Cope, Pte Gavican, Pte Bush and Pte Waters.

Maj Gen Purdon, GOC Nearelf, presents the GOC's Commendation to LCpl Gilley for his gallant behaviour during the fire at Athna Forest refugee camp, observed by RSM Brown standing on the right.

Built under the direction of Maj Jones, OC B Coy, Fort Bravo provided an excellent view of Turkish-held Athna village and was a source of great comfort to local Greek Cypriots: while Ken Howard was working on this painting, OC C Coy persuaded him to change the company flag, much to Maj Jones's irritation!

blast while leading a patrol in Athna Forest. Lance-Corporal Gilley was awarded the Commander-in-Chief's Commendation for his courageous actions during a fire, also at Athna Forest. Lieutenant Hodgson and the Assault Pioneer Platoon accompanied a Royal Engineer Squadron to Nicosia to carry out repairs on the airport, which had been badly damaged during the invasion. They were made 'unofficial' members of the UN, complete with blue berets, but, since they were only engaged on this task for twenty-seven days, they were ineligible for a UN medal.

Belize *Spearhead* Emergency Deployment

In August 1975 the 1st Battalion returned to Gillingham, where it took its turn acting as *Spearhead*, which meant that it should be prepared to go anywhere and do anything, at very short notice. Although British Honduras had recently become independent as Belize, there were few signs of any shift in Guatemalan attitudes. On 4 November B Company (Major Jones) flew out, followed five days later by A Company (Major Coate), each taking their Support Platoon elements with them. While B Company secured the International Airport, A Company deployed to Belmopan. Along with Harriers and a modest Royal Navy presence, this impressively swift response was sufficiently purposeful to discourage the Guatemalans. Both companies were home in time for Christmas – just!

Ex *Peer Gynt*, held on Dartmoor in October 1975, was a multi-phase section test exercise, including casevac by a *Sioux* helicopter.

KAPE (Keep the Army in the Public Eye) tours, the exercising of Freedom rights and Cadet Training Teams were all vital elements in strengthening county links: LCpl Harrison is working with local cadets at Poole in the summer of 1976.

In late 1975 A and C Coys deployed to Belize (which had been known as British Honduras until June 1973) on Op *Spearhead:* this *Land Rover* appears to have reached its limit of exploitation on a challenging jungle route recce.

Digging in to protect Belize International Airport: no amount of insect repellent is going to keep away those aerial 'stingers'!

Chapter 9

The Wider Regimental Family and TA

1967-1977

*B*etween 1967 and 1977 the accelerating pace of change put considerable pressure on the backbone of the British Army: the Regimental system. Training was rationalised: Wyvern Barracks, Exeter, the home of the Wessex Brigade Depot until 1968, when it became the Prince of Wales's Division Depot, closed in 1974. The Depot then moved to Crickhowell in Wales before further rationalisation sent adult recruits to Lichfield for their training, while junior soldiers remained at Crickhowell. The Depot's move from Exeter to Crickhowell was a particular blow since it brought Regular Infantry representation in the two counties to an end. The TA battalions of The Devonshire and The Dorset Regiments were disbanded on 31 March 1967. This weakened the military presence in the two counties, although C Company, The Wessex Volunteers, in Dorchester and E Company, The Wessex Volunteers, in Exeter maintained the highest standards, with the Regiment still supplying the permanent staff instructors.

In 1967 the Regimental Associations of the two former Regiments and that of The

The laying-up of the Dorset Regiment (TA) Colours, Sherborne Abbey, 11 March 1967: (left to right) Lt Col Elford, the Colonel-in-Chief, The Duchess of Kent, and the new Colonel of the Regiment, Brig 'Speedy' Bredin. In the background are WO2 Ellis and WO2 McNaught.

The laying-up of the Devonshire Regiment (TA) Colours, Exeter Cathedral, Easter Monday, 27 March 1967: Lord Roborough, Lord Lieutenant for Devon, takes the salute at the Guildhall.

The Dorset Regimental Association Standard Bearers at Dorchester War Memorial, 9 September 1967: this was an important ceremony of remembrance and part of the Annual Reunion.

The Mayor of Exeter, Alderman Board, talks to members of Devon ACF at the Guildhall, spring 1968: fifty cadets were invited to a reception at which the many trophies won during the previous year were handed over for safekeeping.

Col Cope, who had commanded 2 Devon until mid-April 1918, but handed over to Lt Col Anderson-Morshead just before the Bois des Buttes battle, visited the 1st Battalion in Germany as part of the 50th Anniversary commemorations: he is talking with LCpl Nicholls and Cpl Beale.

On 14 September 1968 the Dorset Old Comrades' Association held a Reunion and Drumhead Service on the square of the old Regimental Depot at Dorchester: over fifty veterans of the First World War were present that day.

Devonshire and Dorset Regiment were still running in parallel. Prior to 1972 the Half Day's Pay Scheme contributions were allocated solely to Devon and Dorset Welfare Funds. From that year onwards twenty per cent of the total was donated to the two old Associations, since the number of their members in need of assistance was steadily increasing. In 1974 the first Devonshire and Dorset Regimental Association reunion took place in Exeter.

The disbandment of the Wessex Brigade meant that, from 1970 onwards, the Regiment was able to wear its own cap badge. That same year the Freedoms granted to the two former Regiments were transferred to The Devonshire and Dorset Regiment. After the first 'active service' casualties in Northern Ireland, there was strong support for a Devonshire and Dorset Regimental Chapel, which was established in the Chapel of St James and St Thomas, Exeter Cathedral in June 1974. New Rolls of Honour, kneelers worked by Regimental wives and wartime plaques recovered from Malta after independence all contributed towards a strong Regimental identity. The Devonshire Regiment Chapel, also in Exeter Cathedral, and the Dorset Regiment Chapel in Sherborne Abbey were both retained. Regimental memorials were a source of constant concern: the 2 Dorset memorial at

In July 1971 Maj Anstey, OC E Coy, 1 Wessex, won the Queen's Medal at Bisley: he was the best shot in the Territorial Army and, over a twenty-year period, enjoyed tremendous success in competition shooting.

Kohima was in a poor state of repair by 1973 while that to 2 Devon at Bois des Buttes in France had to be re-sited as a result of a road-building programme. These – and many other matters – were the responsibility of an over-stretched RHQ staff.

Platoons at the Wessex Depot at Wyvern Barracks, Exeter were traditionally named after Regimental Battle Honours: Ladysmith Platoon passed out in summer 1971 and were fortunate that Tommy Alsford, a 93 year-old veteran, was able to bring the events of the siege of Ladysmith in 1900 alive for them, using the Regiment's Ladysmith gun as a prop.

In the middle of 1975 two stalwarts of Devon ACF, with long service in the TA as well, give up their responsibilities: Col Harrison (left) handed over as Commandant while Lt Col Wheeler (right) retired as Deputy Commandant.

Surrounded by distinguished Dorset Old Comrades, Mr Avery, custodian of the Dorset Military Museum, holds the Commander-in-Chief's Certificate of Commendation for Highly Meritorious Service, which had just been presented to him by the Lord Lieutenant, Col Sir Joseph Weld: among those attending were Brig Bredin (left) and Lt Col Wakely, Assistant Regimental Secretary (second from right).

Presentation of Colours to the 1st Battalion, The Wessex Regiment, 1973: (left to right) Maj Rimmer, Col Roberts, Honorary Colonel, Gen Sir Basil Eugster, who made the presentation, Lt Taylor carrying the Queen's Colour and 2Lt Evans carrying the Regimental Colour. 1 Wessex was formed from the Devonshire Regiment (TA) and the Dorset Regiment (TA).

On 27 May 1968 forty-five survivors of Bois des Buttes formed up on Bury Meadow before a service in Exeter Cathedral to commemorate the 50th Anniversary of that desperate battle. Despite offering fierce resistance under their Commanding Officer, Lt Col Anderson-Morshead, who is seen directing operations in the painting, 2 Devon were finally overwhelmed: just 40 out of a total strength of almost 600 officers and men regained the British lines. The French honoured the Regiment with the award of the Croix de Guerre, a distinction proudly worn by The Devonshire and Dorset Regiment.

Chapter 10

Osnabrück

(including North Belfast 1977 and Central Belfast 1979)

1976-1980

In May 1976 the 1st Battalion took over Belfast Barracks in Osnabrück, less than seven years after leaving the city for Malta. The Battalion was now part of Task Force Delta, the re-named 12 Brigade, part of 2 Armoured Division. On 16 June the Battalion gave welcoming parties in all the messes, preceded by a Beating Retreat spectacularly set before a backdrop of Fort Marabout, which commemorated the unique battle honour earned by the 54th Foot in Egypt in 1801. Then it was straight into the mechanised role once again, with training on the local Achmer training area. This was followed by field-firing at Sennelager, and then deployment to Soltau for

Waiting for the order to move off from the square at Belfast Barracks, Osnabrück: Ex *Quick Train,* which was activated without warning, obliged the Battalion to deploy within two hours to hide positions in the West German countryside.

Four *AFV 432s* of 1 Pl, A Coy advance through the churned mud of Soltau Training area, with a *Chieftain* main battle tank leading the way.

experience in all-arms work, the companies becoming combat teams and the Battalion the core of a battle group. This hurried introduction was put to the test on Ex *Cool Gin* that September when the 1st Battalion battle group participated in a US Airborne/British TAVR/20 Armoured Brigade exercise near Hildesheim. That autumn attention turned once again towards yet another Op *Banner* tour, to North Belfast this time. The six-week training 'package' started in November with briefings by NITAT, platoon and company-based training and specialist range work, culminating in two weeks at Sennelager facing rioting mobs in 'Tin City'. In mid-December the final preparations were witnessed by that determined and regular visitor, Brigadier Bredin.

Maj Wilsey, OC B Coy, on the radio from his *AF* *432* while Pte Dowling wonders which way he wi be asked to turn next.

In the back of Bn Tac HQ's specially-equipped *AFV 432*, Capt Richardson, Ops Officer (left), and Capt White, Adjutant, give radio orders for the next phase of Ex *Cool Gin*, West Germany, September 1976.

In 1976 the 1st Battalion's Bisley Team came a respectable 19th out of a total of 62 major unit teams, improving to 11th the following year: they include (left to right) Lt Thornburn, CSgt Gove, Cpl Ash, Cpl Brookes (REME), Cpl Morton, LCpl Williams, LCpl Cleverly, LCpl Warren and Pte Mountney.

North Belfast, 1977

On 20 January 1977 the 1st Battalion assumed responsibility for a number of strategically-positioned bases in North Belfast. The tactical area of responsibility (TAOR) included the Shankhill, Ardoyne, New Lodge, Unity Flats, Tiger Bay, Old Park-Cliftonville and Ligoniel and there was no shortage of representation from hard-line elements on both sides of the sectarian divide. A Company (Major Field) and C Company (Major Reid) shared Flax Street Mill with HQ Company; B Company (Major Wilsey) was based at the rather more salubrious Girdwood Park while Support Company (Major Turrall) was at Dunmoor. There was no time to take stock of the situation. Within two hours of the handover A Company had to deal with a partially detonated bomb and a bomb under a prison officer's car – the Crumlin Road Jail was in their 'patch'. A later incident involved the successful interception of a hijacked bus, with terrorists and a 10lb bomb on board. In one of many shooting incidents during those early weeks Lance-Corporal Harvey was wounded. For the soldiers it was a seemingly never-ending stream of patient patrolling and observation tasks. This was where the West Country approach – a combination of firmness, fairness and common decency – slowly drove a wedge between those who lived for violence and those who dreamed of a return to normality. Great emphasis was placed on the continuity of observation in the overt OPs in New Lodge and Ardoyne and the use of covert OPs by all companies, which enabled the Battalion increasingly to dominate its TAOR and achieve some notable successes.

After eight years of conflict the terrorists had become increasingly sophisticated:

On 18 December 1976 the outgoing Colonel of the Regiment, Brig Bredin, was dined out by the Warrant Officers' and Sergeants' Mess: back row (left to right) WO2 Spiller, WO2 Hunt, WO2 Blake, WO2 Jarrett; third row (left to right) WO2 Burrlock, WO2 Coker, WO2 (RQMS) Wilding, WO2 Fowler, WO2 Gove; second row (left to right) WO2 Stannard, WO2 Sheersmith, WO2 Willey, WO2 Gallwey, WO2 Walters; front row (left to right) WO1 Barry, RSM Brown, Brig Bredin, BM Garrity, Lt Col Shortis.

It pays to advertise: including (left to right) Cpl Beazer, Pte Hiscox and Lt Startin.

The CO, Lt Col Shortis, greets Mrs Margaret Thatcher, then Leader of the Opposition, when she visits Bn Tac HQ, which was based at North Queen Street RUC Station, with Mr Killen, RUC Divisional Commander, and his Deputy standing behind them.

In January 1977 the 1st Battalion began its fourth Op *Banner* tour, this time in North Belfast: Pte Reade (left) and Pte McCullough of C Coy keeping their eyes open for any suspicious activity in the Ardoyne.

"Just as I was about to issue a parking ticket!": Maj Martin, 2IC, observes the dramatic result of a car bomb that exploded outside the Crumlin Road Gaol.

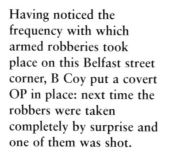

Having noticed the frequency with which armed robberies took place on this Belfast street corner, B Coy put a covert OP in place: next time the robbers were taken completely by surprise and one of them was shot.

sharp-eyed snipers with weapons that could be broken down and hidden in seconds; 'come-ons' designed to lure the Army and the Royal Ulster Constabulary (RUC) into a trap; and well-coordinated, multiple incidents calculated to cause maximum disruption. These had to be – and were – matched by the 1st Battalion's methods. On 19 February 1977, 8 Platoon exchanged fire with a number of gunmen and the rapid follow-up discovered both the firing point and also a secondary device that there had been insufficient time to prime. On 9 March two men ran from a suspect car in the Crumlin Road into the 'safety' of the Ardoyne. A Company immediately cordoned-off the area, although an RUC man was wounded in the process. C Company's OPs spotted three suspicious persons in Dunedin Park and guided foot patrols into the area, leading to a number of arrests and the discovery of two firing points, ammunition and explosives. From the Parlour OP activity by a 'known' group of people aroused suspicion: a foot patrol was directed to the area, arrests were made and a weapon recovered. On another occasion the discovery of a weapon in a garage, followed by a patient stake-out operation, led to an arrest as a man came to collect it. The tour ended in May and members of the 1st Battalion received the following awards: an OBE for Lieutenant Colonel Shortis, Mentions in Despatches for Major Reid and Major Wilsey and a GOC's Commendation for Sergeant McColl.

The Battalion Intelligence Section, under Capt Collett and Lt Biles, was boosted in number for the Op *Banner* tour in Belfast, and some of them even made a vague effort to blend into the local scene: back row (left to right) LCpl Mears, Best, Guppy, Gardiner, Knight, Fuller, Short; middle row (left to right) LCpl Sinclair, Cpl Ali, Thompson, Thomas, Peake, Griffen; front row (left to right) CSgt Barrett, Sgt Kendrick, C/Sgt Jellard, Lt Biles, Capt Collett, WO2 Jarrett, Sgt Jones, Sgt McGowan.

HRH The Duke of Kent, who was appointed Colonel-in-Chief the previous year, pays his first visit to the 1st Battalion, in Osnabrück, on 19 April 1978: he is seen here with, from left, Lt Beresford, Lt Col Bullocke, CO, and Pte Bray who is carrying the new *Clansman* radio.

On returning to Osnabrück, the *Sarah Sands* march-and-shoot Competition soon tested fitness and military skills that might have become slightly rusty: 3 Pl certainly look as if they have been put through their paces. Platoon members include (left to right) Cpl Lambert, Cpl Helliwell, LCpl Hincke, Sgt Riley, Pte Guppy, Pte Davey, Pte Braddon 56, Pte Mulqueen.

Ex *Medicine Man* was the name given to all-arms, live-firing battle group-level exercises that took place on a rotational basis at Suffield on the Canadian prairie from spring through to autumn: this platoon from A Coy has leaguered up and is checking ammunition, fuel, etc., summer 1978.

Ex *Medicine Man*: *AFV 432s* advance to contact across the blazing prairie. Every so often exercises would grind to a halt as soldiers put out the fires.

Ex *Medicine Man*: after a long day an *AFV 432* and its tired crew are silhouetted against the setting sun.

A team from B Coy marched from Osnabrück to Plymouth in order to raise money for charity and were given a civic welcome at the Keep in Dorchester: (left to right)) LCpl Mooney, LCpl Strickland, the Mayor of Bridport, Lt Col Wakely, Assistant Regimental Secretary, Pte Laine, the Mayor of Dorchester, LCpl Russell.

Osnabrück

Back in Osnabrück, the 1st Battalion was at last able to focus on its BAOR role. There was a succession of training cadres, CPXs, border patrols and site guards, typically of nuclear installations. Lieutenant Colonel Bill Bullocke took over from Lieutenant Colonel Shortis in June 1977 and, shortly afterwards, it was announced that HRH The Duke of Kent had been appointed as our Colonel-in-Chief, a position that had been vacant since the death of his mother nine years earlier. The long-awaited refurbishment of Belfast Barracks commenced on the Battalion's return from leave, leaving many to wonder why it hadn't started when everyone was otherwise engaged in Ireland. Although there was considerable disruption to the soldiers' domestic arrangements, the

In front of competitors and spectators, Sgt Bennett holds aloft the *Victor Ludorum* trophy that he won at the Battalion Sports Day, Osnabrück, 1978.

The 1st Battalion's fifth Op *Banner* tour, Belfast 1979: the stand-by patrol from 3 Pl is being briefed by LCpl Johnson (third from left), with Pte Woodhouse, Pte Conway and Pte Temme.

For security reasons, access to Belfast City Centre was only possible through the segment gates. A particularly high-powered team are visiting this gate: (left to right) the Adjt, Capt Young, RSM Burrlock and the CO, Lt Col Bullocke.

Pte Aldham and Pte Phillips look in a state of shock, having been standing next to a civilian who was hit by a sniper, in mistake for one of them, at Queen Street segment gate in central Belfast. Behind them Capt Langdon, the Battalion's Press and Media Officer, is busy making a report.

Shades of Bob Monkhouse and *The Golden Shot:* a BBC cameraman shouts 'left a bit' to Pte Jones in order to obtain the perfect composition.

On operational tours it was customary for the 1st Battalion to choose a suitable pin-up to adorn walls, lockers and notebooks: *Miss 1 D and D*, Georgie Steer, is seen with (left to right) Pte Cridge, LCpl Murphy, Pte Ward and Pte Mills.

Three 'pigs' advance towards a group of rioters: soldiers are dismounting from the lead vehicle in order to disperse the crowds.

Back at Belfast Barracks, Osnabrück, the training cadres got under way once again: Sgt Duff inspects LCpl Fuller as the Junior NCO's Cadre prepare for a day of section attacks.

end result was a move away from Victorian conditions (actually a pre-war German cavalry barracks) to something approaching late twentieth-century comfort. In September the Battalion spent ten days field-firing at Sennelager while the support platoons – Mortars and Anti-tanks – did the equivalent at Munsterlager.

This was useful preparation for the annual *Sarah Sands* march-and-shoot, which took place on 4 October, after which C Company departed for Soltau and a gruelling work-up for Ex *Medicine Man* in Canada as part of 5 Inniskilling Dragoon Guards Battle Group. The 1st Battalion Battle Group also went to Soltau that autumn. It comprised A and B Companies, the Mortar and Anti-tank Platoons, the tanks of B Squadron, 5 Inniskilling Dragoon Guards, Forward Observation Parties from 7 Royal Horse Artillery, Armoured Engineers and *Swingfire* anti-tank and *Blowpipe* anti-aircraft sections – in all some 700 men and 150 armoured vehicles. All-arms co-operation was the order of the day and the Battle Group was put to the test in Ex *Keystone*, which took place south of Münster.

In the new year the Battalion reorganised onto the '650' establishment. The support platoons went to HQ Company, leading to a company strength of no less than 370, while D Company came into being. There was also new technology as the *Clansman*

The Colonel of the Regiment, Gen Archer, talking to members of B Coy during a visit to the ranges at Sennelager in 1979: Pte Evans knows the answer to the question and has his hand up first, watched by (right) Capt Thornburn and CSM Henderson.

The Government Taxation Office in Ormeau Avenue gushes smoke after an incendiary device explodes: while shootings were rare on this tour, high profile targets such as this were frequently bombed.

series of radios were issued for the first time. D Company (Major Dutton) received its first test on exercise with the Dutch Air Force in early March. That winter almost 200 soldiers were able to take part in Ex *Snow Queen*, a popular introduction to downhill and langlauf skiing. On 19 April 1978 HRH The Duke of Kent paid his first visit as Colonel-in-Chief, accompanied by the new Colonel of the Regiment, General Sir John Archer. Battalion HQ and A Company immediately started training for Ex *Medicine Man* 4, for which they took two squadrons of 5 Inniskilling Dragoon Guards under command. Preparations at Soltau were followed by the unrivalled experience of field-firing and manoeuvre on the Canadian prairie while the exercise concluded with adventurous training and a few days of 'rest and recuperation' (R and R). The other companies were not left out completely: B Company (Major Stone) attended the

Officers and Senior NCOs of A Coy, Osnabrück, autumn 1979: (left to right) WO2 Jellard, Lt Randle, Sgt Lambert, Capt Archer, Sgt Duff, Maj Steptoe, Sgt Madders, Lt Underhill, Sgt Beazer, 2Lt Hill (on attachment from the Australian Army), Sgt Maybry, CSgt Morgan, WO2 Westlake.

French Commando School on Ex *Bold Barracuda*; C Company (Major Delves) carried out dismounted training in the Eiffel Mountains while D Company administered the 2 Armoured Division Mortar Concentration at Munsterlager, joined Battalion HQ at Soltau and, finally, went to La Courtine in France for dismounted work. The last mechanised training that year was Ex *Certain Shield*, a two-week reinforcement exercise for US forces in the Frankfurt area that also involved British Task Force Delta and German, Dutch, Belgian and Luxembourg units. The annual *Sarah Sands* march-and-shoot competition was won that year by 3 Platoon (Lieutenant Archer). From the end of September it was back into the now-familiar Northern Ireland, Op *Banner*, training routine.

Central Belfast, 1979
The 1st Battalion's Main Body arrived in Belfast on 13 January 1979. A and D Companies had merged into City Centre Company (Major Dutton) and was based, together with Battalion HQ, in the faded grandeur of the Grand Central Hotel; B Company (Major Cooper) spent three months at North Queen Street RUC Station before moving to Girdwood Park while C Company (Major Pook) found itself back in Flax Street Mill, after an interval of less than 18 months. Access to Belfast city centre

was controlled by segment gates: everybody who passed through had their identities checked and there were frequent searches. The purpose of this manpower-intensive task was to convince a nervous population that it was possible to live and work normally in the centre of Belfast. Outside the gates, shootings and bombings persisted, but they were less frequent than on previous Northern Ireland tours. This tour saw the introduction of much more widespread surveillance, both overt and covert, over the whole Battalion area. The Close Observation Platoon (Major Delves) played an important role in these developments.

Incidents included C Company's cordon and subsequent checking on 23 January of a suspect car that had been used in two earlier murders; a shooting incident at one of the segment gates; a follow-up operation by C Company after the murder of Prison Officer Makin and his wife on 4 February; a search on 13 February that unearthed 500 rounds, weapon sights and silencers; the careful dispersion, on 1 March, of thirteen bombs round the city to 'mark' the ending of political status for IRA prisoners and the targeting of banks using incendiary devices on 22 March. There were a series of incendiary attacks in April, culminating in a devastating one on the Tax Office on the 26th. There was a view that almost anybody might wish to claim responsibility for that one! Visitors to the 1st Battalion during the four-month period included the Bishop of Sherborne, the Chief of the General Staff and the Colonel of the Regiment, while the press descended in force on central Belfast for Margaret Thatcher's election victory on

The 1st Battalion's Orienteering Team won the 2 Armoured Division Championships, Rehburge Wald, spring 1980: back row (left to right) Capt Archer, Capt Biles, Maj Pook, Lt Harrison, Cpl Kelsall; front row Cpl Drake and Lt Underhill.

3 May 1979. With the tour almost over, a 200lb bomb exploded on 11 May, shattering an estimated 4,000 windows. The following day a member of the RUC was shot and wounded, south of the City Hall: the getaway car was quickly found in the adjacent Markets area. While quieter than previous Op *Banner* tours, there could be no let-up in the need for constant vigilance. As a result of the tour, there was an OBE for Lieutenant Colonel Bullocke, Mentions in Despatches for Major Dutton and Major Delves and GOC's Commendations for WO2 Henderson, Sergeant Titley and Lance-Corporal Smith.

Osnabrück

On 13 May 1979 the Battalion returned to Osnabrück and, after leave, yet more training. Train hard, fight easy! Everyone went to Sennelager for field-firing and the Colonel of the Regiment paid another visit. The Anti-tank Platoon did extremely well to win the 1st British Corps Concentration at Putlos, something they had first achieved a dozen years earlier. After Sennelager the Devon and Dorset Battle Group (less D Company, which had gone to Canada with the 5 Inniskilling Dragoon Guards Battle Group), including the tanks of B Squadron, 5 Royal Inniskilling Dragoon Guards, the armoured recce of B Squadron, 1 Royal Tank Regiment, 129 Battery of 40 Field Regiment RA, 21 Light Air Defence Battery and a Troop of 37 Engineer Squadron went to Soltau, where they were visited by the Chief of the Defence Staff. A two-week work-up preceded Ex *Keystone*, during which the Battle Group rehearsed all phases of war, including no less than three crossings of the River Weser. That autumn the *Sarah Sands* march-and-shoot competition was won by 7

Janner, the 1st Battalion's semi-official newspaper

Platoon (Lt Rundle). In December 1979 Lieutenant Colonel John Wilsey assumed command from Lieutenant Colonel Bullocke. The ability of the determined terrorist to strike almost at will was exemplified by the shooting by the IRA, on 10 March 1980, of Lance-Corporal Sims while he was running in local woods. Fortunately he survived, having managed to reach hospital before collapsing.

Chapter 11

Colchester

(including Armagh 1981
and Kenya 1982)

1980-1983

The 1st Battalion arrived at Roman Barracks, Colchester in April to join 7 Field Force, formerly 19 Infantry Brigade, and soon to be so designated once again. While in Germany the pattern of life was determined by the BAOR training cycle and the demands of higher formation exercises. Life in the air-portable role in Colchester would be rather less complex, with the additional benefit of re-establishing links with the two counties. On 12 June 1980 there was a visit from the Colonel-in-Chief, during which he presented Lance Corporal Sims with a GOC's Commendation and inaugurated the 'Duke of Kent's Platoon Competition'. At the end of the month the Battalion embarked on a two-week KAPE tour: A Company (Major Steptoe) was based in Dorset, B Company (Major Jefferies) in Plymouth, C Company (Major Pook) in Exeter and D Company (Major Shaw) in Barnstaple. There was a parade to exercise the Freedom of Exeter on 5 July and another one to receive the Freedom of Christchurch on 9 July.

WO2 Henderson jumped over a two-foot wall, not realising there was a ten-foot drop the other side: *Miss Westward*, Jane Hooley, obligingly signs his plaster but doesn't seem to be bringing tears to his eyes.

Sgt Williams of the Mortar Pl, aided by the RAF Loadmaster and the local farmer, trying to devise a strategy to rescue a drowning bullock.

Now that the bullock has become an honorary member of the Mortar Pl, it will be encouraged to 'bed in' properly in future!

The bullock looks extremely uncomfortable as a rather unusual under-slung load for a Royal Air Force helicopter.

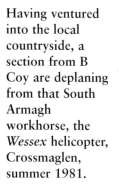

Having ventured into the local countryside, a section from B Coy are deplaning from that South Armagh workhorse, the *Wessex* helicopter, Crossmaglen, summer 1981.

On 12 September 1981 the IRA attempted a mortar attack on the RUC Station at Bessbrook: fortunately an explosion in the cab of the hijacked lorry – believed to be the self-destruct device – failed to detonate approximately 400lbs of home-made explosive on the flat bed.

Ex *Crusader* was the largest British Army deployment since the end of the Second World War. After extensive study of the operational concepts, there were a series of Battalion exercises including, *Thirty-Nine Steps*, *Janners' Shield* and *Red Panther*. Ex *Crusader* itself involved several phases: *Spearpoint* was the 1 (BR) Corps field exercise, *Jog Trot* and *Canoe* involved reinforcement from the UK while *Square Leg* was the mobilisation of T&AVR for home defence. The trip to Zeebrugge, on requisitioned Danish ferries, was memorable for the comment from a number of soldiers that 'the prawns were a bit crunchy'. Apparently no-one had explained that they tasted better if peeled before consumption! In mid-September the 1st Battalion took up its *Goodwood* position, south of Hanover. *Spearpoint* had four phases; aggressive delay, a defensive battle, withdrawal and, finally, a counter-attack. In many respects Ex *Crusader* was too large and complex, either to

Maj Gen Gerrard-Wright, GOC Eastern District, presents Long Service and Good Conduct medals: (left to right) Cpl Reade, Cpl Marriott, Sgt Bates and WO2 Henderson.

challenge, or even constructively to occupy, the more junior ranks – it was never to be repeated.

Inter-Mess Tug-of-War, Colchester, summer 1980: RSM Wilding oversees another thrashing of a struggling Officers' Mess by the Warrant Officers' and Sergeants' Mess. Officers' Team Coach Capt Beresford tries to rally his men, who include Lt Underhill, Maj Steptoe, Capt Biles, Lt Col Wilsey, Capt Whitfield and Maj Collings.

The 1st Battalion ran out winners of the Eastern District Athletic Championships in 1982: Brigadier McCord, Deputy Commander, Eastern District, presents the team prize: (left to right) LCpl Rawlinson, Capt Nicholls, WO1 (RSM) Jellard, LCpl Saunders, Sgt Lock, WO2 MacPherson and Pte Gidley.

Novice Boxing Tournament winners, Colchester 1982: Maj Langdon, OC A Coy, with Cpl Beresford, team coach, sitting on his right.

The new Colours march past and dip in slow time as the Colonel-in-Chief salutes in response, 22 May 1982: Lt Clayden (Queen's Colour), WO2 Westlake, Lt Watson (Regimental Colour), escorted by CSgt Peters and CSgt Williams 90.

On 22 May 1982 the Colonel-in-Chief presented new Colours to the 1st Battalion, replacing the first stand, which had been carried for the previous twenty years: Lt Beattie and Lt Toomey march off the old Colours.

After the formality of the Colours Presentation, it was time for a traditional 'ox roast': SQMS Connor had been keeping a careful eye on developments for the previous two days to ensure that it was done to a 'T'.

The 1st Battalion's very own 'Wurzels' get the party off to a flying start, Colours Presentation, Colchester, 22 May 1982: (left to right) Sgt Underwood, Cpl Potter, SSgt Dyer and Sgt Read.

Before Christmas the annual *Sarah Sands* march-and-shoot competition took place and was won by 10 Platoon (Lieutenant Saunders). On 6 January 1981 Wagon Hill Day was celebrated in the traditional way with the Warrant Officers and Sergeants thrashing the Officers at rugby, followed by drinks for all in the Officers' Mess and the Warrant Officers staying for a Dinner Night. The next Northern Ireland tour was put back four months to July, enabling sport to return to the agenda with the Battalion Football Team reaching the final of the Infantry Cup. As a result of the Battalion's high manning levels, recruiting restrictions were imposed, leading the CO to carry out a revealing survey. It transpired that forty-two per cent of the Battalion had family connections; that seventy-nine per cent lived in, or on the boundaries of, either Devon or Dorset (of those three-quarters were from Devon and a quarter from Dorset) and seventy-one per cent had been educated at schools, colleges or universities within the two counties. Every officer satisfied one or more of these criteria while a quarter of all ranks had fathers, or close family members, who had served in the Regiment, or one of its predecessors. It was an impressive demonstration of what it means to belong to a family regiment.

Armagh, 1981

The next Op *Banner* deployment, this time to Armagh, commenced on 26 July 1981. The 1st Battalion's operational area included over sixty miles of border, parts of two RUC Divisions (H and K) and 560 square miles of territory. With two companies attached from resident battalions, there were six companies permanently under command. Battalion HQ, HQ Company, A Company (Major Thornburn) and the Close Observation Platoon were based at Bessbrook; B Company (Major Jefferies) was at Crossmaglen; D Company (Major Shaw) was at Middletown and Keady while C Company (Major Collings) acted as patrol company, also based at Bessbrook. Helicopters or covert road movement took the foot patrols to their areas of operation in countryside that was still deceptive and threatening. On 31 July an RUC car was blown-up and, five days later, there were a number of Province-wide bomb incidents, including cross-border 'Action Sunday', an IRA-inspired attempt to drum up support for Maze hunger strikers, which turned out to be something of a damp squib. On 1 September 1981 Lance-Corporal Dempsey and Private Hulley were blown off their feet, but not seriously hurt, by an explosion on the Castleblaney Road. On 26 September Corporal Gardiner engaged gunmen taking up position on a school roof in Ardross Estate but, despite his vigilance, hot pursuit failed to secure any arrests. On 7 November a tractor bomb exploded in Crossmaglen and eight civilians were injured. On 18 November Lance-Corporal Hutt and Private Bissett were wounded in an exchange of fire with gunmen whose van they had fortunately spotted manoeuvring suspiciously. Constant, professional suppressive patrols, both overt and covert, reduced the IRA's freedom of action and boosted confidence among the local people. The list of awards tells the story of a job well done in the highest traditions of the Regiment: an MBE for Major Collings,

Mentions in Despatches for Lieutenant Colonel Wilsey, Major Jefferies, Captain Burrlock, WOII Thompson, and Corporal Hutt, and GOC's Commendations for Master Chef WO2 Connor, Corporal Parmenter, Corporal Dempsey and Lance-Corporal Taverner.

Colchester

The Battalion returned to Colchester on 11 December 1981 and, after leave, it was straight into training cadres, both for Junior NCOs and also for Section Commanders' Tactics. Time was found for the annual *Sarah Sands* march-and-shoot, won this time by 6 Platoon (2nd Lieutenant Backhouse) while the General Purpose Machine-Gunners achieved third place in the newly-resurrected, Army-wide, Machine-Gun Cup at Warminster. On 22 May 1982 the Colonel-in-Chief presented new Colours to the 1st Battalion at Roman Barracks. It was a memorable parade that took place in front of thousands of invited guests and formed a fitting conclusion to Lieutenant Colonel Wilsey's period in command. On 4 June he handed over to Lieutenant Colonel Paddy King-Fretts.

Meanwhile, in the South Atlantic, both former and serving members of the Regiment were distinguishing themselves. On 28 May 1982 Lieutenant Colonel Jones, formerly OC B Company but now commanding 2 Para, was killed at the head of his men during the Battle for Goose Green, demonstrating gallantry for which he was subsequently awarded a posthumous Victoria Cross. All three Regimental

When the sad news came through that Lt Col H Jones, formerly of the Regiment, had been killed while in command of 2 Para in the Falklands, there was a moving Service of Remembrance on the square at Roman Barracks, Colchester.

A Family Regiment

Colin, David and Philip Lane

John and Jeremy Archer

Charlie and Martin King

David, Rupert and H Jones

Haydn and Don Jellard

Robert and Rupert Steptoe

Sam and David Steevenson

Speedy and David Bredin

Kenny and Ken Marshall

Ted and Paul Harris

John Wright and John, Junior

A Family Regiment

Alexis and Dickie Turrall

Andrew and Jamie Edwards

Will and John Randle

Justin, Janner and Dean Westlake

Steve and Ernie Peters

Jack and David Harrison

Guy, Simon and Rod Young

John, Nick and Robin White

Ron and Paul Gavican

Inter-company Boxing Competition 1980: Maj Steptoe (right) wearing old-style Mess kit; back row (left to right) Lt Backhouse, Capt Archer, Lt Harrison, Lt Blewett.

Lt Col Wilsey, on giving up command of the 1st Battalion, is pulled out of camp in a traditional West Country vehicle, 4 June 1982: (left to right) Capt Steevenson, Maj James, Capt Gaye, accompanied by the 'Wurzels' on the trailer.

Junior NCO's Cadre final exercise, Dartmoor, December 1980: "Is it really worth going through this agony just to get my first stripe?"

representatives who took part in that short, sharp conflict received gallantry awards: Major Delves, who would later become Colonel of the Regiment, was awarded the DSO for his leadership of D Squadron, 22 SAS, including the assault on Pebble Island, while Petty Officer John Leake, NAAFI Canteen Manager on HMS *Ardent*, who had served with the 1st Battalion in Northern Ireland and volunteered as a Petty Officer just six days earlier, brought his Army experience to bear and was awarded the DSM for damaging an Argentinian *Skyhawk* so badly with a machine-gun that it crashed on attempting to land at Port Stanley. On 16 October 1982 Exeter Cathedral was full when a moving service was held in memory of Lieutenant Colonel H Jones VC OBE.

That autumn the 1st Battalion was fortunate to return to Kenya on Ex *Grand Prix*. For six weeks the Battalion enjoyed live-firing at Mpala Farm, dry training at Dol Dol, jungle work at Gathiuru and indirect live-firing at Archer's Post, ending with a test exercise. There were opportunities for adventurous training in the Aberdares, at Meru, on Mount Kenya and in the Masai Mara, together with well-earned 'R and R' at Lake Naivasha, Mombasa and Lake Turkana. The only sadness was that eleven members of the Mortar Platoon were injured in a road accident and had to be evacuated to the UK. The Battalion returned from Kenya on 7 December and, after Christmas leave, the next three months were spent preparing for a period as a resident battalion in Northern Ireland, which would be very different from the now-familiar Op *Banner* tours.

Several members of the Mortar Pl were seriously injured in an accident involving this *Bedford* 4-ton vehicle while on exercise in Kenya in November 1982: they included Pte Bounden (who, though still paralysed, is Captain and Secretary of Otters Wheelchair Basketball Club), Sgt Darragh, Sgt Warren and Sgt Larvin.

The 1st Battalion Rugby Team won the Eastern District Championship three years running: back row (left to right) Pte Austin, Dmr Wood, LCpl Berry, LCpl Edgcumbe, LCpl Phillips, Pte Hunter, Pte Edy, Pte Smith, Pte Marland, Pte Tunnicliffe, Pte Eveleigh, LCpl Allen, Pte Thursman; front row (left to right) Lt Wallace, Lt Beattie, SSI Reynolds (APTC), WO1 Jellard, Lt Col King-Fretts, Maj Langdon, D/Maj Cox, Lt Dyer, Capt Trevis.

The Duke of Kent's Competition Cup is presented by Lt Col King-Fretts, the new CO, to Lt Mollison, who led 1 Pl to victory.

With roads poor or non-existent, it was left to the mule train to carry the water supply to the troops, Kenya 1982: CSgt Keane and Pte Lane 93 set off for B Coy's location.

Chapter 12

The Wider Regimental Family and TA
1977-1984

*W*hen the 1st Battalion was based outside the UK, or on unaccompanied operational tours, it was the responsibility of the Colonel of the Regiment and his deputies, RHQ and others – serving or retired – in the two counties to help maintain the Regiment's high profile. There was frequent contact with the Lords Lieutenant, with the Mayors and other civic dignitaries, with HMS *Devonshire* (until she was decommissioned in July 1978), with HMS Exeter (commissioned in

These members of C Coy, 1 Wessex, based in Dorchester, have just been presented with medals and Certificates by the Lord Lieutenant of Dorset, 1977: back row (left to right) Sgt Chivers, LCpl Burt, Pte Topp; front row (left to right) WO2 Gould, WO2 Price, Maj Speakman (Coy Comd), CSgt Denty and LCpl Larcombe.

Heavily-laden cadets from B Coy, based in Plymouth, look nervous, but excited, about the challenges that lie ahead of them on the *Ten Tors Challenge* 1977.

September 1980), with RAF Chivenor, and also with our affiliated regiments in Canada, Australia and Malaya. The two ACFs and the school CCFs were also part of this wider Regimental family. The key to the success of RHQ was having the right people on the spot: people who knew the Regiment well and were committed to the task in hand. In this respect the Regiment has always been extremely fortunate.

On 7 February 1997 General Sir John Archer succeeded Brigadier 'Speedy' Bredin as Colonel of the Regiment while, the same year, Brigadier Randle took over as Regimental Secretary, based in Exeter, from Lieutenant Colonel Windeatt. In September 1979 Lieutenant Colonel Wakely retired as Assistant Regimental Secretary and Museum Curator at Dorchester and was replaced by Major Wyllie, who had previously been in Exeter, while Lieutenant Colonel Stone became Assistant Regimental Secretary in Exeter. An important development during this period was the amalgamation of the Welfare Funds of the three Regimental Associations, which took place in 1979. Meanwhile the Territorial Army remained unusually stable and C and E Companies, 1 Wessex, continued to be a credit to the Regiment: for example, these two companies provided the backbone of the 1 Wessex team that won the prestigious China Cup, the major unit trophy for shooting, in both 1979 and 1982. On 1 December 1979 Colonel Michael Bullock succeeded General Sir John Archer as Colonel of the Regiment, handing over in his turn to Major General Colin Shortis in December 1984.

In May 1978 just nine survivors of the battle were fit enough to travel to France to celebrate the 60th Anniversary of Bois des Buttes: (left to right) Messrs Wickham MM, Clarkson, Bone, Prout, Paramor, Bryant, Westlake, Hewett and Bonetta.

In May 1978 the 2 Devon Memorial at Bois des Buttes was moved and rededicated: a Colour Party from the 1st Battalion (left to right) Lt Gray (Queen's Colour), Sgt Dunn, CSgt Riley, Lt Saunders (Regimental Colour) and Sgt Cox, together with a Guard of Honour from the French Army, march past the Parade Commander, Maj Field, watched by veterans of the battle.

The Devon and Dorset companies from 1 Wessex had an extremely successful year on the range in 1979: the outstanding competitor was Cpl Price, who won the Queen's Medal with a score of 564, no less than 44 points clear of his nearest rival.

1 Wessex Shooting Team with the China Cup, Bisley 1979: Lt Col Southwood, the CO (third from right), is seen with the team members: Lt Cook, Sgt Hendrick, CSgt Purshouse, Sgt Chivers (whose father had been in the 4 Dorset team that won the China Cup in 1956), Cpl Price, Cpl Stainer, LCpl Turner, LCpl Daden and Pte Upshall.

There was a service to dedicate new furnishings in The Devonshire and Dorset Regimental Chapel of St James and St Thomas in Exeter Cathedral on 22 March 1980: the tapestry kneelers were worked by Lady Archer, Mrs Sara Jones, Mrs Susan King and Mrs Peggy Randle, while the stained glass window depicts St Alban, the soldier saint, with the Regimental Badge in the roundel and the arms of the two counties in the side lancets.

On 9 July 1980 the Regiment was granted the Freedom of the Borough of Christchurch, which had become part of Dorset after the local government reorganisation of 1974: Col Michael Bullock, the new Colonel of the Regiment, and Mrs Kathleen Bullock (right) are pictured with the Mayor of Christchurch, Councillor Bishop, and Mrs Bishop.

The Dorset Regiment was granted the Freedom of Lyme Regis on 16 August 1945, the first town to honour the County Regiment in this way. During a KAPE Tour in July 1980 the right to march through the town 'with bayonets fixed, drums beating and Colours flying' was exercised by A Coy: Maj Steptoe leads the way, followed by (among many others) Capt Randle, WO2 Jellard, LCpl Philips, Pte Dibble, Pte Hunter, Pte Glanfield and Pte Stockley.

On 19 September 1980 the Band of the 1st Battalion (on the left) represented the Regiment at the commissioning ceremony for HMS *Exeter*, our affiliated Royal Navy ship.

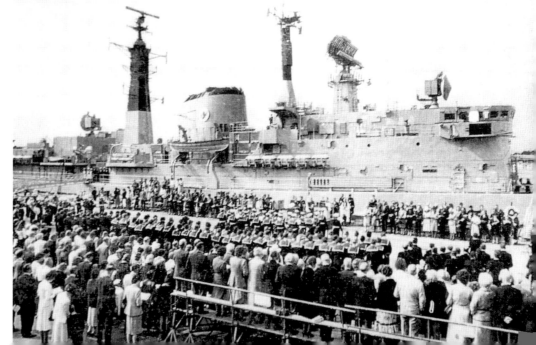

Brig Shortis visits the Regiment's representatives at the Infantry Junior Leaders Battalion, Shorncliffe, Kent: Maj Rogers (Coy Comd) and Lt Barnes (Pl Comd) stand on his left in the back row. Among the Junior Leaders themselves are Jnr Sgt (later Capt) Skinner (standing, left), Jnr Ldr (later Capt QGM and bar) Gillespie (kneeling second from right) and Jnr Ldrs Darnell, Bailey, Woodward, Bailey-Burnley and Dobbs.

Having visited the 1st Battalion on operations in South Armagh in the autumn of 1981, the Lord Mayor of Plymouth, Councillor Morrell, generously hosted a reception in Plymouth for the wives and families of local members of the Regiment.

Chapter 13

Ballykinler

1983-1985

By 24 March 1983 the 1st Battalion was installed at Abercorn Barracks, Ballykinler. This was a good barracks, providing you inclined more towards nature and water-sports than night-life! Ballykinler is delightfully rural with the sands of Dundrum Bay and the Mourne Mountains sweeping down to the sea. The challenges faced by a 'resident' battalion on a two-year tour are very different from those confronting units on an Op *Banner* tour. The latter tend to have a distinct TAOR and work sixteen hours a day, seven days a week, unaccompanied by their families. For resident battalions the operational intensity can be just as great, while deployment can

The team from C Coy won the 1st Battalion Shooting Competition, Ballykinler, 25/26 April 1983: back row (left to right) Sgt Kelsall, LCpl Buckland, Pte Shaw, Pte Stevens, Pte Shears; front row (left to right) Pte Symns, Pte Daniels, Sgt Latham, Pte Taylor and LCpl Mills.

Lt Col King-Fretts and WO2 Beale inspect the 1st Battalion ACF Detachment, presenting cap badges (for slightly outsize berets in some cases), 23 June 1983: Cadets Beale, Conway, Easton and Westlake subsequently joined the 1st Battalion.

Cpl Pritlove puts enthusiastic young members of the 1st Battalion Judo Club through their paces for the benefit of two visiting Members of Parliament: (left) David Harris, MP for St Ives, who was commissioned as a National Service officer into The Devonshire and Dorset Regiment in 1958 and (right) Tony Speller, MP for North Devon, who served with 1 Devon 1952-54.

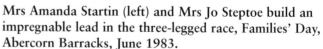

Mrs Jill Burston and Mrs Lyn Jellard achieve the right balance between competition and enjoyment during the greasy pole event, Families' Day, Abercorn Barracks, June 1983.

Mrs Amanda Startin (left) and Mrs Jo Steptoe build an impregnable lead in the three-legged race, Families' Day, Abercorn Barracks, June 1983.

take place anywhere within the Province. At the same time it is essential to preserve normal life as far as is possible although families' freedom to shop and travel are naturally limited by security factors. Thus resident battalions are more self-contained and independent. Their sub-units, companies and platoons, form a strategic reserve, deploying as and when needed. Initially one company from the 1st Battalion was based in Belfast but that commitment later ceased and a company was sent to Bessbrook in Armagh instead.

On 28 March D Company (Major Pape) went to Belfast, under the command of 1 Black Watch. Just two days later Corporal Jeffrey was critically wounded in a bomb attack in the Falls Road. Immediate care, both at the scene and later at the Royal Victoria Hospital, was of no avail and he died of his wounds on 7 April 1983. The company providing security at Ballykinler also formed a Quick Reaction Force (QRF).

WO2 Crawford (second from left) calls D (Sp) Coy smartly to attention: those on parade include Cpl Spencer, Cpl Warren and LCpl Allen.

B Company's QRF was deployed as early as 26 March in response to shots being fired at Castlewellan RUC station. In the days that followed B Company (Major White) also provided platoons for search operations under the command of 3 UDR. On 24 April A Company (Major Langdon) went to Belfast for six weeks. On 8 May 9 Platoon from C Company (Major Hambrook) was working with a Royal Marines patrol when the latter drove into an ambush on the Kilkeel-Rostrevor Road. Fortunately the 700lb device only partially exploded and there were no injuries. A 9 Platoon foot patrol, in a swift follow-up, closed on the scene from the Rostrevor Forest Park, just failing to cut the terrorists' escape route. On 24 May a proxy bomb was left in a van outside Andersonstown Police Station. The explosion severely damaged the station and blew several members of an A Company patrol off their feet; they just dusted themselves down and carried on with the job. For the General Election on 9 June 1983 B and C Companies provided guards on polling stations. That autumn many members of the 1st Battalion were involved in trying to recapture thirty-eight members of the IRA who escaped from the Maze Prison on 25 September: while half were apprehended within a few days, some never returned to prison. On 27 October 1983 C Company was under the command of 1 Grenadier Guards in South Armagh when Lance-Corporal Taverner was caught in a bomb explosion in Crossmaglen and died in the Queen Elizabeth Military Hospital at Woolwich a week later.

RQMS Tucker shows HQ Coy veterans the way during the annual Combat Fitness Test: the group includes Pte Forte, Cpl Clift, LCpl Kelly and Cpl Larvin.

The 1st Battalion Cricket Team, 1984: they include, back row (left to right) Sgt Pook, Pte Lousteau, Lt Toomey, Pte Holmes, Pte Berry, Pte Runyard; front row (left to right) LCpl Berry, LCpl Ruddock, Capt Harrison, Lt Startin, Lt Field.

LCpl Bridgeman collects empty water bottles while the rest of the patrol, which includes Cpl Connolly and Pte Hay, sort themselves out before the next phase of the *Cambrian March Patrol Competition* in 1984.

Oman

A particular highlight of the Ballykinler tour was a six-week company field training exercise in Oman in February/March 1984. With the Parachute Regiment unable to take part, Ex *Rocky Lance 3* was offered to the 1st Battalion. A composite company group under the command of Major Pape was formed for the exercise and the Mortar and Milan Platoons  were joined by a composite rifle platoon. The exercise was based at Tathi on the IZZ Range Area near the old capital of Oman, Nizwa, with a live field-firing package based at the Saiq Range Area, high up on the Jebel Akhdar. During the first phase all three platoons undertook a pre-dawn march up the precipitous Wadi Muaydin from Birkat Al Mawz to Saiq, the route taken by assaulting SAS troops some 30 years previously during the Jebel Akhdar operation. The next phase gave each platoon the opportunity for live-firing while the final phase was a three-day company tactical exercise against a live enemy, which culminated in a company attack, supported by the Mortar and *Milan* Platoons, *Jaguars* from the Sultan of Oman's Air Force and a battery of 105mm guns from the Oman Artillery Regiment.

Ballykinler provided plenty of opportunities for non-military activities. Within a few

A highlight of the Ballykinler tour, for those fortunate enough to go, was Ex *Rocky Lance* 3, which took place in Oman in February/March 1984: members of the Atk Pl appear in this photograph (left to right) Pte Austin, LCpl Brown, Pte Squires and Cpl Smith 42.

During Ex *Rocky Lance* 3, D (Sp) Coy held a Tug of War competition: LCpl Cormack and Sgt Toogood on the rope, supported by Cpl Marshall, Cpl Ali, Lt Toomey, Pte Furzeman, Cpl Allen and Capt Barnes.

months of arrival no less than 150 Devon and Dorset children were wearing uniform, with the Army Cadets, Scouts, Guides, Cubs and Brownies forming thriving groups, all staffed by members of the Battalion or their wives. Meanwhile the Saddle Club had a large following, the cricket team was flourishing, while water sports included canoeing, wind-surfing, dinghy sailing and water-skiing. Thus was normality maintained in an environment where the threat was seldom very far away. Lieutenant Colonel Bryan Dutton took over as CO from Lieutenant Colonel King-Fretts on 23 October 1984. That winter Regimental traditions were maintained, including the Warrant Officers and Sergeants holding a *Sarah Sands* Ball, and the normal commemoration of Wagon Hill on 6 January. On 8 March 1985 there was a reflective occasion as the Very Reverend Robin Eames, Archbishop of Armagh, dedicated a bell in memory of Corporal Jeffery and Lance-Corporal Taverner. Representatives of their immediate families – Mrs Jeffery and Mr and Mrs Taverner – were present at a moving service that took place in the Garrison Church of St Martin in the Mournes. To mark the Regiment's Tercentenary – the raising of the Duke of Beaufort's Musketeers, the 11th (North Devonshire) Regiment of Foot, in June 1685 to combat Monmouth's Rebellion – there was a Freedom March through Exeter, followed by a service in Exeter Cathedral for the laying-up of the first stand of Devonshire and Dorset

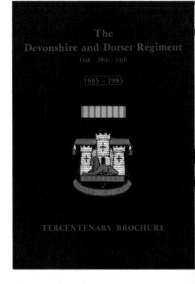

Regiment Colours. On 23 March 1985 the officers celebrated with a Tercentenary Ball at Ugbrooke House, the home of Lord and Lady Clifford of Chudleigh. Thoughts then turned to the next posting, to the British zone of a still-divided Berlin.

Ballykinler was not all deployments and guard duties: here are members of the 1st Battalion Saddle Club (left to right) Maxine Peters on *Kelso*, Pte Peters on *Sandy*, Maj Pape on *Devon Lad*, Josie Kirby on *Amber*, Chrissie Hutt on *Ranger* and Carl Peters on *Buttons*.

The 1st Battalion expedition to the Swiss Alps after ascending the Eiger by the West Ridge: Capt Sharpe, Capt Watson, Pte Richardson, Pte Smith 21, Pte Bell and Pte Whiteley.

The 1st Battalion Rugby Team take the game to their opponents, 7 RHA: (left to right) LCpl Smith 21, Lt Jellard, LCpl Bridgeman, Cpl Stocks and Pte Tunnicliffe.

Four tired but elated soldiers are welcomed and congratulated by Jimmy 'Jim'll Fix It' Savile after marching 500 miles in order to raise money for the Stoke Mandeville Appeal Fund: (left to right) Pte Garlinge, Pte Edwards, LCpl Schnur and Pte Morris.

The Memorial Bell at St Martin's in the Mournes Garrison Church at Ballykinler is dedicated to the memory of Cpl Jeffery and LCpl Taverner, both of whom were killed in 1983 when the 1st Battalion was based at Abercorn Barracks, Ballykinler. Plans are in progress to centralise at Ballykinler the memorials to all those members of the Regiment who have died in Northern Ireland.

Tin hats on – tin hats off – tin hats gone! 5 Pl reach out for the finish line, H Jones Competition, 1984: (left to right) Pte Tucker, Pte Brooks, Pte Dumbleton, Pte Newcombe 37, Pte Lousteau and Pte Fox.

Chapter 14

Berlin

1985-1987

$\mathcal{A}$t the end of the Second World War Berlin was divided into four sectors – Russian, French, American and British – with the city itself marooned 100 miles within Communist East Germany. Road and rail access to Berlin from West Germany was through controlled corridors, which remained under the threat of arbitrary closure by the East Germans, depending on the international situation. These factors combined to make Berlin something of a showpiece for the western democracies. Inward investment was huge, the standard of living was very high and, for military personnel stationed there, the job was extremely high profile. It was vital that military training and exercises, constant guard duties and frequent parades demonstrated the British Army's resolve and professionalism. Whether on or off duty, military personnel in Berlin were never out of the public eye. The 1st Battalion moved into Brooke Barracks in April 1985. Familiarisation with the new role included border patrols, providing observers on the military train,

Success for the 1st Battalion 7-a-side Hockey Team: back row (left to right) 2Lt Jones, Lt Field, LCpl Sharp, 2Lt Storrie; front row (left to right) Maj Dewar, Cpl Collis, Pte Lousteau.

visits to both parts of the divided city, preparations for the summer parade 'season' and, as a welcome contrast to Ballykinler, a taste of night life!

Tired members of A Coy hitch a much-appreciated lift on a *Chieftain* main battle tank: traversing the turret might cause a problem or two!

On 7 June 1985 the Queen's Birthday Parade took place on the Maifeld, used by the Nazis for May Day parades and also for polo matches and gymnastics displays during the 1936 Olympics, in front of HRH The Prince of Wales and some 20,000 spectators. Just a week later there was a celebration of the Regiment's Tercentenary with a drumhead service, a street party and sports in the afternoon. Seven days after that came Allied Forces Day Parade, with representatives of the three Allied occupying forces marching from the Brandenburger Tor, past the Siegessäule, or Victory Column, along Strasse-des-17 Juni. The 1st Battalion led the British contingent, almost exactly 40 years

As part of the Berlin Tattoo, the Band and Drums of the 1st Battalion dressed as 'Pearly Kings' performed for the crowds in front of the Reichstag.

The Allied Forces Day Parade passes the saluting base on Strasse-des-17 Juni, with the Siegessäule (Victory Column) in the background: CSgt Burston leads the *Fox* armoured cars of the 1st Battalion's Recce Pl.

The 1st Battalion played 1 Royal Hampshires in the BAOR Cricket Competition, 29 June 1985: they include, back row Cpl Ruddock, Lt Harrison; middle row (left to right) Cpl Berry, Pte Holmes, Pte Berry, Pte Lousteau; front row (left to right) Maj Young, Maj Rogers, 2Lt Field, Maj Dewar.

Specialist equipment for a specialist role: this *AFV 432* Mk II is fitted with a 30mm *Rarden* cannon. Note that the FIBUA role in Berlin also necessitated different camouflage in order to break up the vehicle's outline.

A *Fox* armoured car from the 1st Bn moves away from the Berlin Wall.

WO2 Bates receiving his prize from the CO, Lt Col Dutton, at the Inter-Company Athletics Competition: Maj Bridge announces the winners, watched intently by LCpl Holmes, LCpl Glanfield, LCpl Harris, LCpl Town and Sgt Braddon 42.

Berlin Brigade Boxing Final: a battle-scarred Pte Backhouse launches an impressive counter-attack against Pte Mitchell.

The Aslt Pnrs became experienced in core skills such as preparing the major bridges for demolition: Pte Polkey lays a 'hayrick' cutting charge.

The back blast is hard to disguise as a *Wombat* of the Atk Pl fires at Bergen-Hohne Ranges: LCpl Lousteau, Det Comd, with his No 1 and No 2 at the gun.

after 2 Devon had marched along the same route at the Allies' 1945 Victory Parade. The next major public occasion was Charlottenburg Friendship Day on 31 August for which each Army unit in Berlin was affiliated to a civilian district and organised Janner-inspired entertainments, which included climbing the greasy pole, bowling for a pig and tossing the hay bale.

After all these public commitments the 1st Battalion spent the first three weeks of September in Schleswig-Holstein on Ex *Green Bear*, which involved some real infantry soldiering. The pace quickened from platoon training, to company tactics and a 50-mile march, before concluding with a Battalion exercise covering many phases of the infantryman's war: attack, defence, patrolling and helicopter assault. This was an essential preparation for the Berlin Brigade's Ex *Hungry Bear*, which took place at Soltau two months later. One of the more mundane tasks undertaken on a regular basis by members of the Battalion was the provision of a guard for Spandau Prison, where Rudolf Hess was by now the sole survivor of the seven Nazis imprisoned there after the Nuremburg War Crimes Trials. When Hess died on 17 August 1987, having been the only inmate for the previous twenty-one years, the British authorities swiftly demolished Spandau Prison in order to prevent it becoming a shrine to Nazism.

The following February a Brigade call out, testing Berlin Garrison's readiness to deploy on operations, acted as a precursor for the next training season, field-firing at Sennelager and the end of an era as the anti-tank *Wombat* was fired for the last time at the Brigade Skill-at-Arms Meeting. In July there was a ceremony commemorating the 70th Anniversary of the start of the Battle of the Somme: the 1st Battalion provided a Guard and the Regimental Band from Berlin while many Old Comrades visited from the UK. Following the main commemoration at Thiépval, the Colonel-in-Chief and the Regimental contingent repaired to Mametz, where a service was held to dedicate a replacement memorial at Devonshire Cemetery, one of the most moving on the Western

On 9 June 1986 the 1st Battalion's first
female Assistant Adjutant, 2Lt Hewitt,
inspects the guard, accompanied by Sgt
Lewis of the Orderly Room.

For the annual Queen's
Birthday Parade the 1st
Battalion provided No 3
and No 4 Guards: with the
Parade drawn up on Berlin'
Maifeld, 7 Flight, AAC
thrill the crowds with a
dramatic fly-past.

With the sporting calendar
unavoidably disrupted by
inclement weather, there
was an impromptu
Snowman Competition: (le
to right) Pte Allen, Cpl
Sheppard, L/Cpl Houston,
Pte James, Pte Burton, Pte
Huston, Pte McManus and
Pte Phillips.

Members of the Wives' Club prepare to launch themselves on an unsuspecting world in Ex *Petticoat*, **a night exercise in the Grünewald.**

Front. No less than seven battalions from both Regiments had fought in those desperate battles in 1916: 1, 2, 8 and 9 Devon and 1, 5 and 6 Dorset. The original wooden memorial, which marked the old front line trench of 8 Devon and 9 Devon, in which those who fell there on 1st July 1916 were buried, had decayed. A fine Portland stone replacement still bears the proud words: 'The Devonshires Held This Trench … The Devonshires Hold It Still'.

It was the parade season that distinguished Berlin from the 1st Battalion's other postings. In 1986 the now-familiar annual parades were supplemented by a visit from the Colonel-in-Chief on 21 July and the Berlin Tattoo on 25 September. For the latter the 1st Battalion performed a colourful re-enactment of the Battle of Plassey on 23 June 1757, as a result of which the Regiment acquired the unique battle honour of Plassey and the title 'Primus in Indis', or First in India. The Berliners were somewhat bemused by the degree of realism injected by the use of elephants from Berlin Zoo! Ex *Green Bear*, another regular feature of the Berlin training cycle, took place in Schleswig-Holstein that November, and provided another opportunity for the Battalion to escape the rather claustrophobic atmosphere of Berlin. The curtain was now coming down on a challenging and interesting tour in a city on the cusp of change, although that wasn't so obvious at the time. Less than three years later the tearing-down of the Berlin Wall would be the catalyst for the collapse of European Communism: the two halves of the city were reunited after forty-eight years of forced separation and Berlin would once more be the capital of a greater Germany.

The nature of the Berlin commitment meant that the 1st Battalion had to become proficient in FIBUA skills.

Between 31 March and 4 April 1986 a series of teams from the 1st Battalion took part in a Multi-Marathon, running from Berlin to Exeter: back row (left to right) LCpl Scott, Pte Hale, Cfn Lilly, Pte Corbin, Cpl Finch; front row (left to right) Pte Brailey, LCpl Jerrard, Pte Holloway, LCpl Laws, Sgt Williams, LCpl Osborne. Other runners were Pte Moreland, Pte Harris and Pte Croft.

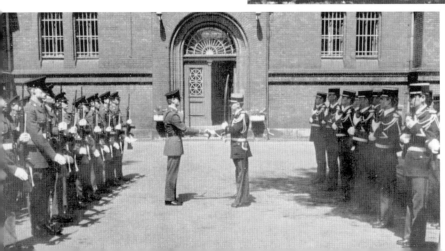

Lt Terry and a Guard provided by the 1st Battalion hand over their Spandau Prison duties to the French Army.

Chapter 15

Bulford

(including Falkland Islands 1987, Belize 1988, Denmark 1988, Kenya 1989, Armagh 1989 and United States 1990)

1987-1991

The 1st Battalion took over Kiwi Barracks, Bulford in February 1987. Although the barrack blocks were in a poor state compared with those in Berlin, there were compensations in the excellent local training facilities and, of course, the proximity to the two counties. At the same time Lieutenant Colonel David Shaw took over command from Lieutenant Colonel Dutton. The Battalion was now part of the United Kingdom Mobile Force (UKMF), or 1 Infantry Brigade, which had a varied and challenging role that demanded great flexibility from its constituent units. The Battalion was soon on *Spearhead* stand-by and, with problems developing in far-flung places such as Fiji and the Lebanon, as well as more prosaic Northern Ireland, a call-out seemed highly probable. In the event the 1st Battalion was not required and, once the *Spearhead* commitment had ceased, the re-establishment of West Country links became a priority. There were Freedom Marches through Weymouth and Dorchester and visits from civic dignitaries and the ACFs of both counties.

All of a sudden the 1st Battalion was inundated with new 'kit' – the *Light Support Weapon (LSW)*, a new helmet, the wheeled *Saxon* 'armoured taxi' and *Land Rovers* 90 and 110: LCpl MacManus and LCpl Dibble clearly think it is Christmas as they unwrap an *LSW*.

In Op *Roger* the 1st Battalion was tasked with the protection of American *Cruise* missiles from angry demonstrators: the Battalion laid more than 10 kms of *Dannet* wire when the missiles were deployed to Salisbury Plain from the controversial US air base at Greenham Common, near Newbury.

On 19 March 1988 the Regiment received the Freedom of the City of Plymouth, the largest city in the two counties: Colour Party, Lt Brock and Lt Paddock; Escorts to the Colours, WO2 Hincke, CSgt Kelsall and CSgt Braddon 56.

The badge of The Devonshire Regiment was carved into the chalk downland above the village of Fovant, Wiltshire, in 1916: the badge requires constant maintenance, which is being carried out here by Cpl Davey and other volunteers from Sp Coy.

Maj Biles, OC C Coy, enjoys a moment of peace and quiet on Onion Ranges in the Falkland Islands.

During the Falklands Tour, the Recce Pl deployed to South Georgia under the command of Maj Trevis: back row (left to right) Sgt Coath, Sgt Henderson, Sgt Harrison; front row (left to right) WO2 Fitzgerald, Maj Trevis, Sgt Lee, Lt Warren.

Falkland Islands, 1987

Elements of the Battalion reinforced the Falklands Islands Garrison during the last half of 1987. C Company (Major Biles) was responsible for securing the airfield at Mount Pleasant, providing a Quick Reaction Force and sending patrols to visit the outlying settlements, where their reassuring presence was much appreciated. The Recce Platoon (Major Trevis) went to South Georgia and, having been dropped off by HMS *Dunbarton Castle*, received supplies and mail by parachute every two weeks. Their compensation for this hardship was that they were able to practise winter warfare tactics and snow and ice

The newly-arrived Night Observation Device, or NOD, is put to the test – it looks disturbingly similar to the smoke grenade launchers on the turret in the background.

The wheeled *Saxons* were first used when the 1st Battalion deployed to Denmark on Ex *Bold Grouse*: the bicycles seen on the roof came in useful when radio silence had been imposed.

Despite advances in technology affecting almost every other aspect of Army life, potatoes are still peeled the same old way: Cpl Burton demonstrates the well-tested technique.

climbing in a harsh, but unforgettable, environment. There were also opportunities to enjoy the wildlife and make thought-provoking visits to the battle sites from the 1982 campaign.

Those left in Bulford had the unenviable task of guarding Greenham Common, the controversial USAF base where *Cruise* missiles were stored. By February 1988 the Battalion began to be re-equipped with *Saxon* and B Company (Major Gaye) went to Stanford for familiarisation training. Meanwhile A Company (Major King) went to Belize on Ex *Mopan Shield*, a rapid reinforcement that took place in January and February. Having moved south for an uncomfortable 12 hours by road, A Company acted as enemy for Ex *Toucan Blade*. They were then left to carry out their own training at Baldy Beacon, English Caye and in various jungle locations – in incessant rain. At the end there were a few days of much-needed 'R and R', enabling many soldiers to go to Mexico or Miami.

While training in Kenya, A Coy came across the 39th camel – but couldn't find the 11th or the 54th anywhere!

A Company returned to the UK just in time for the H Jones Competition, which took place in Wales that March. For three days patrols of ten – each platoon providing two patrols – were put through a series of military tests while navigating an arduous route in singularly unpleasant weather. This Competition was particularly poignant since, not only had the participants recently returned from the Falklands, but Mrs Sara Jones presented the prizes. On 19 March 1988 the Regiment received the Freedom of Plymouth, with the 1st and 4th Battalions, the Old Comrades and Devon ACF on parade. In April the 1st

The resupply and refurbishment of the OPs in South Armagh took place during Op *Tantalus:* the helipad at Bessbrook is extremely busy with a *Chinook* landing in the background and *Puma*, *Wessex* and *Gazelle* helicopters in the foreground.

Control of the helicopters at Beesbrook was the responsibility of the Buzzard crew: among their number were Sgt Kershaw (APTC), Sgt Strickland and Sgt Braddon 42.

Maj Harding, the Paymaster, Padre Rutherford and SSgt Porter, REME, are among those 'volunteers' on sandbag-filling duty with HQ Coy.

A group from the 1st Battalion, led by WO2 Williams, return by *Chinook* to Bessbrook in South Armagh after a welcome spell of 'R and R'.

The IRA attacked the Glasdrumman OP with four remotely-controlled mortar bombs concealed in the link box of a tractor: fortunately it veered off course and no-one was hurt. Each mortar bomb, though home-made and unpredictable, was a fearsome projectile weighing over 30 pounds.

Battalion ran Ex *Test Match* on Salisbury Plain, followed by 1 Brigade's Ex *Wiltshire Pheasant*, which was the debut of the *Saxons*, a wheeled but rather ineffective APC. For three weeks in September, the 1st Battalion deployed on Ex *Bold Grouse*, UKMF's biennial exercise, for which some 5,000 men, with their vehicles and equipment, were moved by land, sea and air to Zealand in Denmark. The heli-borne assault on Bogo was memorable, as were the defensive battles against Danish and German 'enemy' parachute drops and counter-attacks in the *Saxons*. The

Ex *Trumpet Dance* took place at Huckleberry Creek Mountain Training Centre, Washington State, USA in early 1990: back row (left to right) Sgt Wills, Sgt Haycock, Maj Randle, WO2 Bell, Cpl Christie, American host, Lt Paddock; front row (left to right) Sgt Hilton, Lt Hunt.

final battle was observed by sixty members of the multi-national inspection team, including senior Soviet officers, reflecting reduced East/West tensions.

On returning to Bulford the 1st Battalion was once again *Spearhead* battalion. This time it was an attempted coup in the Maldives that November that caused international concern; however, the sun cream purchased in anticipation of a visit to those coral atolls in the South Seas wasn't needed on that occasion! In the event A Company was despatched to less-than-exotic Nesscliffe to do some preparatory work for the next Op *Banner* tour while Support Company (Major Hambrook) reformed as a rifle company. Early in 1989 the Battalion made another very satisfying, month-long deployment to Kenya for the now-familiar routine of field-firing, exercises, adventure training and 'R and R'. After returning from Kenya, preparations began for another four-month Op *Banner* tour in South Armagh.

Armagh, 1989

The 1st Battalion assumed responsibility for South Armagh on 12 April 1989 with A Company (Major King) at Forkhill, C Company (Major Hale) at Newtownhamilton and Support Company (Major Hambrook) at Crossmaglen. B Company (Major Trevis), Battalion HQ and Echelon were based at Bessbrook. On the face of it, little had changed. The same RUC liaison officer was sitting in the same chair, and greeted the new arrivals with a cheery: "Good to see you back, chaps!" The Commanding Officer's stated objective was to 'leave the situation better than we had found it'. B Company rotated through the Airborne Reaction Force (ARF) on a four-day cycle and provided 'multiple' patrols. The other companies patrolled their TAORs incessantly. During the early weeks several IEDs (Improvised Explosive Devices) were found on the Dublin-Belfast railway line, leading to lengthy clearance operations. A particular

The Band was subject to quinquennial inspections by team from the Royal Military School Music at Kneller Hall: the 1st Battalion Band, seen here being put through their paces by Band Sergeant Major Read, achieved a excellent result in 1990.

On a visit to Kiwi Barracks, Bulford, the Colonel-in-Chief tal with (left to right) RQMS Balcombe, Sgt Barrett REME an Sgt Larvin in the Warrant Officer and Sergeants' Mess.

Maj Gen Jeapes, GOC South-West District and formerly of the Regiment, has just presented Long Service and Good Conduct medals to (left to right) Sgt O'Rourke, Cpl Rose and Sgt Clift.

Our affiliated Royal Navy ship, HMS *Exeter*, frequently hosted members of the Regiment: Lt Bates, CSgt Winter, LCpl Partiss and others brave the English Channel, December 1989.

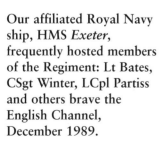

This time the regular Friday cross-country run really was across – as well as over – the country: (left to right) Cpl Woods, WO2 Young, Cpl Austin, Cpl Rees, LCpl Fox, LCpl Moody, Cpl Edmunds and LCpl Vinicombe.

challenge was Op *Tantalus*, a major refurbishment of Security Force bases, since it was difficult to disguise the routine movements of those involved. Sadly Corporal McGonigle of C Company, 1 Worcester and Sherwood Foresters, who was temporarily attached to the 1st Battalion, was killed by a roadside bomb. The Colonel-in-Chief visited on 28 July 1989, staying for lunch at Bessbrook. A month later everyone was back in Bulford, the Battalion's eighth tour in Ulster had come to an end and the general view was that South Armagh had been left 'better than we had found it'.

The return to Bulford coincided with a change of Commanding Officer as Lieutenant Colonel Chris Biles took over from Lieutenant Colonel Shaw. That autumn had a familiar feel to it: the *Sarah Sands* march-and-shoot, numerous sporting

The Band of the 1st Battalion are photographed at Bulford on 1 November 1990 before they deployed as part of Op *Granby* to Kuwait, where they were to join 33 Field Hospital, acting as medics and stretcher bearers: they include, back row (left to right) Sgt Pritlove, LCpl Symes, Cpl Oliver, WO1 (Bmr) Perry, Cpl Mitchell, CSgt O'Brien, Cpl Cross, Cpl Chugg, Cpl Davies; front row (left to right), Bdsm Boase, LCpl Wilds, LCpl Wilson.

competitions and a KAPE tour that included Freedom Marches through Torbay on 13 October 1989 and through Plymouth the following day. That November the CO instituted a 'Special Act of Remembrance' with the names of all those members of the Regiment killed on operations being read out. This has since become the central feature of the Battalion's Remembrance Sunday Service. On 19 January 1990 the Colonel of the Regiment watched the traditional Wagon Hill rugby match, which had been delayed in his honour.

On 26 February the advance party arrived in Washington State for Ex *Trumpet Dance*, a short but very busy deployment. There was company-level work at Fort Lewis, Yakima and Huckleberry Creek, followed by a short Battalion exercise and three days' 'R and R'. The splendidly-named 'Daughters

CSgt Mountney demonstrates his waterman capabilities, keeping both his SA80 and his beret dry, during Ex *Janners' Stroll*, which place on Stanford Training Area.

of the British Empire' generously hosted a tea party for 500 while, in return, the Battalion hosted a Beating Retreat and cocktail party at the end of the exercise.

The 1st Battalion was now in its last year at Bulford, well practised in its various roles and experienced at fielding 'fast balls'. The Battalion took its turn again at *Spearhead* that June with Liberia discussed as a possible troublespot. In the event the 'balloon' did not go up and the last field training with UKMF, Ex *Druids Drake*, took place on

During the First Gulf War the 1st Battalion reopened Rollestone Camp on Salisbury Plain at very short notice as a prisoner-of-war camp: within 72 hours the first inmates arrived, with the world's press and representatives from the Red Cross hot on their heels! Fortunately it soon started to snow, driving most of the less welcome visitors away.

An outstanding team from the 1st Battalion won the annual Northern European Command Infantry Competition (NECIC), held in Denmark, beating entries from Denmark, Germany, Norway, Canada and the Netherlands: they include, back row (left to right) Pte Bosley, Pte Kennedy, Pte Redstone, Pte Docherty, Pte Butt, Pte Clements; front row (left to right) Sgt Jerrard, Capt House, Cpl Fitzgerald, Pte Iddon.

Salisbury Plain in July 1990. The most conspicuous feature was a distinct shortage of ammunition. Financial pressures were having an adverse effect on Army training and Ex *Bold Grouse*, the last UKMF exercise of the year, proved to be a tame bird and was cancelled altogether. After summer leave there was a notable achievement as Sergeant Jerrard and his team, trained by Captain House, won the North European Command Infantry Competition in Denmark, beating entries from Denmark, Germany, Norway, Canada and the Netherlands. Following Saddam Hussein's invasion of Kuwait, the Regimental Band, acting in their traditional role as stretcher bearers, went out to Al Jubail, Saudi Arabia on Op *Granby* as part of 33 Field Hospital. Having received excellent training and endured no less than 15 Red NBC alerts in twenty-five days, they returned home on 16 March 1991. Meanwhile, after setting up a prisoner-

of-war camp at Rollestone on Salisbury Plain, the 1st Battalion joined 5 Airborne Brigade on Ex *Fast Buzzard*, fully expecting to take part in an operation to recapture Kuwait City, but the call never came. After intensive training courses for conversion to the new APC, *Warrior*, the Battalion departed for Werl in Germany in early August 1991. Although there was much talk of the 'peace dividend' as the Warsaw Pact disintegrated, the 1st Battalion was fortunate to have secured another high-profile and purposeful role.

Ex *Bold Grouse 3*: a group of officers puzzling over the carcass of a tent, which doesn't appear to have come with clear, *Ikea*-style instructions for erection: Maj McKenzie Johnson, Lt Bates and Maj King.

The Drums practise the *Last Post*, Bulford: they include (left to right) Cpl Hellings, Cpl Phillips, Dmr Davies and Dmr Harris.

Although the 1st Battalion had the honour of being the first unit to use the newly-built FIBUA village on Copehill Down, Salisbury Plain, they had to fill 6,000 sandbags first: (left to right) Pte George, LCpl Crawford and Pte Burt relish the task!

1st Battalion Athletics Meeting, Bulford Stadium, summer 1989: Mrs Liz Biles presents Cpl Griffiths with his winner's medal for the Javelin, watched by (left to right) Capt Titley, Lt Col Biles and Maj Nicholls.

Chapter 16

The Wider Regimental Family and TA

1984-1990

The new Colonel of the Regiment, Major General Colin Shortis, applied his very considerable energies to building on the platform provided by his predecessors and, in the process, greatly strengthened the Regimental structure. In 1986 the Charter of the Regimental Committee was altered and the following year there was a major development: a new Home Defence TA Battalion was to be formed. The project officer, Major Pape, was in place at Butts Road TA Centre, Exeter, by February 1987. Lieutenant Colonel Robert Steptoe, the first Commanding Officer, took up his appointment that October. The new battalion, 4th Battalion, The Devonshire and Dorset Regiment (4 D and D) comprised Battalion HQ and E Company at Exeter, A Company at Plymouth while B Company was split between Paignton and Torbay. In the first instance all the representation was from Devon. In October 1990 this imbalance was addressed when C Company at Dorchester joined from 1 Wessex, thereby creating a footprint in both counties. On 19 March 1988 there was a landmark occasion as

The Colonel-in-Chief arrives at Exeter Cathedral for the Tercentenary Service, where he is greeted by the Dean of Exeter, the Very Reverend Richard Eyre.

the Regiment was granted the Freedom of Plymouth, not only the largest city in either county, but also the Regiment's most fertile recruiting ground. This parade was the first ceremonial commitment for the 4th Battalion while the 1st Battalion, which was now

On 23 March 1985 the Regiment celebrated the Tercentenary of the raising of the 11th Foot, later The Devonshire Regiment, by the Duke of Beaufort: Dorset Regiment Standard Bearers, all of whom are Second World War veterans, march proudly past the saluting base at Exeter's Guildhall.

CSM Kennard threatens Sgt Murphy with extra duties if he doesn't give him his last Rolo!

During a visit to the 1st Battalion, ACF Cadets use a *Saxon* wheeled vehicle as the back-drop for a group photograph.

As part of the Tercentenary Celebrations the first stand of Colours of the 1st Battalion, The Devonshire and Dorset Regiment, which had been presented in 1962, were laid-up in the Regimental Chapel: the Colonel of the Regiment, Maj Gen Shortis, is seen entrusting the Colours to the care of the Dean of Exeter, 23 March 1985.

Almost thirty years after amalgamation the three Regimental Associations combined together to form a single Regimental Association, Vesting Day, Bulford, 14 May 1988: Regimental Association Standard Bearers lead a march past of the Old Comrades.

in Bulford, was also well represented. The previous year the three Regimental Associations, having carefully preserved their separate identities for almost thirty years, agreed that the time had come to form a single Regimental Association. On 14 May 1988 there was a Vesting Day Parade at Bulford during which, symbolically, all three Associations marched on parade separately, before marching off together. The Colonel-in-Chief was present on this historic day, together with over 3,500 members of the Regimental family. The following May the 4th Battalion hosted the first of the now familiar annual Regimental Days, combining a parade, a Service of

As part of Vesting Day, the 1st Battalion put together a series of stands reflecting the Battalion's recent activity: this group is enjoying refreshments in front of the Falklands and South Georgia stand.

This group of Old Comrades takes advantage of a break in the proceedings to enjoy a light lunch, Vesting Day, Bulford, 14 May 1988.

'From tiny acorns, mighty oaks …' The challenging task of raising what was to become the 4th Battalion, The Devonshire and Dorset Regiment was undertaken by Maj Pape (right), Project Officer, and Capt Sharpe, Adjutant designate, seen here at Wyvern Barracks on 3 March 1987. The minibus in the photograph was the first item of equipment they had to sign for!

Very soon the nascent 4th Battalion was inundated with kit, which this group is busily trying to unpack and take on charge: (left to right) RQMS Willey, Sgt Williams, CSgt Convery, LCpl Vale, WO2 Brown (kneeling) and Capt Stacey, QM.

Once the 4th Battalion's infrastructure was firmly in place, a number of companies of the Wessex Regiment (TA) rebadged as Devon and Dorsets: on 10 October 1987 Maj Gen Shortis, as Colonel Commandant, Prince of Wales's Division, presents a new cap badge to Sgt Cusack of 1 Wessex, while Lt Col Pook, CO 1 Wessex, looks on.

The Army Cadet Force detachments, with their dedicated instructors, have always been a fertile recruiting ground for the Regular Army. Members of the Ivybridge Detachment, Devon ACF, are pictured at Knook Camp, Wiltshire in 1987: on the extreme left is Adult Instructor Rawlings, whose wife commanded the Detachment; on the extreme right is Cadet Cpl Boon, who later became an Adult Instructor.

Remembrance, the Colonel of the Regiment's Reception and a reunion, bringing together all elements of the Regimental family.

In 1985 both C and E Companies of 1 Wessex camped at Sennybridge in September. C Company (Major Cook) made a considerable name for themselves on the shooting range. In 1986 both companies went to Denmark on Ex *Bold Guard*, since they were very much part of the UKMF. E Company joined the newly-raised 4th Battalion in 1987 while C Company joined 1 Wessex for camp that year at Sennybridge and, the following year, were back in Denmark again. In 1988 the 4th Battalion went to Okehampton for its first annual camp, which was followed that September by Ex *Drake's Drum*, South-West District's Home Defence exercise. Less than a year into its existence the 4th Battalion already had an excellent reputation although recruiting remained a priority. The Battalion held its Skill-at-Arms Meeting in April, before taking on the responsibility of running South West District's concentration of Home Service Force (HSF) Companies at Sennybridge. The Battalion was raising G (HSF) Company at Plymouth at this time. The highlight of the 1989 was Ex *Summer Sphinx*, a battalion exercise involving FIBUA and heli-borne deployment on Salisbury Plain.

In March 1989 Mrs Eileen Salloway, Mayor of Torbay, one of the Regiment's Freedom Towns, visited the 1st Battalion at Bulford: she is signing the Visitors' Book at the Warrant Officers' and Sergeants' Mess, watched by Sgt Riordan and RSM Titley.

Councillor Blake (left), a member of the Regimental Band, either regular or volunteer, for many years, is seen with Lt Col Cooper (centre), CO of the 4th Battalion, and the Town Crier on the occasion of his 'Mayor Making', Honiton, 1990.

Lieutenant Colonel Charles Cooper assumed command in April 1990 and, when C Company from Dorchester joined on 8 December that year, the 4th Battalion proudly took its place in the Army's order of battle.

From 1985 Lichfield was the Regimental Depot for the training of adult soldiers but Crickhowell closed in 1987 and the training of junior soldiers was centralised at the Junior Infantry Battalion at Shorncliffe. Eventually Lichfield's responsibilities for the training of adults expanded to include TA recruits, potential NCOs and potential officer courses. From the Regimental point of view the real disappointment was that training took place so far from the West Country. As with much of the Army during the late 1980s, the future of Regimental Museums and RHQs had been subjected to considerable scrutiny. In fact it wasn't just these important symbols of Regimental identity that were under threat, it was the very existence of The Devonshire and Dorset Regiment itself. In June 1990 Lieutenant General John Wilsey succeeded Major General Shortis as Colonel of the Regiment. The same year Major Pape succeeded Colonel Tremlett as Regimental Secretary and Lieutenant Colonel Roberts succeeded Lieutenant Colonel Burdick as Assistant Regimental Secretary.

Mrs Peggy McMaster, WRVS, a long-time friend and supporter of the Regiment, is greeted by Sgt Lewis during a visit to the 1st Battalion in Berlin.

Chapter 17

Werl

(including Belfast 1993)

1991-1994

The collapse of Communism and the resulting dissolution of the Warsaw Pact prompted a radical reappraisal of UK defence policy, so-called 'Options for Change'. The implications for British forces in Germany were far-reaching. Three divisions were reduced to just one, which would now become part of the Allied Command Europe (ACE) Rapid Reaction Corps, an international formation under a

When the 1st Battalion arrived in Werl one of the first things that they had to do was respray all the vehicles from Desert Yellow to West Country Green: (left to right) Pte Reid, LCpl Hayman, Pte Cox, Pte Harte and Pte Wheadon.

Before Christmas 1991 the CO, Lt Col Biles, together with the youngest soldier in the 1st Battalion, Pte Pern, make up the mix for the seasonal cake, anxiously watched over by the catering staff.

The armoured infantry role does not preclude traditional foot-soldiering, as Lt Allen and his radio operator, Pte Gidley, find out on this occasion.

The German authorities were naturally concerned about military vehicles leaving mud on civilian roads: CSM Latham is no doubt wondering what he has done to deserve this clearing-up job on Soltau Training Area.

Brig Elliott, Commander 6 Armoured Brigade, escorted by the new CO, Lt Col Young, presents Gulf War medals to some of the 34 members of the Regiment who took part in Op *Granby*: (left to right) LCpl Parsons, LCpl Symms, Pte Johnstone.

On arrival in Werl the Recce Pl was delighted to be issued with tracked *Scimitar* recce vehicles, complete with a 30mm *Rarden* cannon: (left to right) Cpl Conway, Pte Jellis and Cpl Amor.

On 22 July 1992 the Divisional Colonel, Col Shaw, visited the 1st Battalion: (left to right) Sgt Killen, Lt Col Young, Col Shaw.

As the post-Cold War *Options for Change* study led to cuts deeper into the Army establishment, farewell parades became ever more frequent: Cpl Hellings plays at the Draw Down Parade for Soest Garrison.

British commander. The British Army would be reduced in strength from 156,000 to 120,000, leading to redundancy programmes and regimental amalgamations. It was ironic that, just a week after the government's initial announcement on 25 July 1990, Saddam Hussein invaded Kuwait. Nevertheless the die was cast and the government pressed ahead with its reforms after the first Gulf War. In fact British Army strength was soon revised down to 116,000 and, by 1997, had been reduced once again, to just 104,000.

For much of its time at Bulford the 1st Battalion had been equipped with the wheeled *Saxon*, a lightly armoured 'taxi' with limited off-road mobility. The tracked *Warrior* was a quite different proposition with excellent cross-country performance and much better armoured protection than either the *Saxon* or the *AFV 432*, with which the Battalion had been equipped on earlier tours in BAOR. To some extent, *Warrior* could also fight 'closed down' using the *Rarden* 30mm cannon and chain gun. When the Battalion arrived in Werl in August 1991, the *Warriors* were still sand-coloured and battle-scarred from the Gulf War. Effective use of *Warrior* would require both mental adjustment and familiarisation training and, for the rest of the year, the 1st Battalion worked hard to ensure that it was 'fit for role'.

Early in 1992 the Battalion moved en bloc, with the *Warriors* aboard rail flats, to Sennelager for three weeks of intensive exercises. This was an opportunity to put into practice everything that had been learned during the previous four months and the finale was Ex *Rhino Express,* a twenty-mile speed march. There was then hardly time to draw breath back at Werl before everyone went to Soltau for a further three weeks of tactical work-up, accompanied by a squadron from 5 Inniskilling Dragoon Guards and sappers from 26 Engineer Regiment. Once the Soltau phase had been completed,

Even the *Warrior* loses its tracks every now and again: Pte Bending of B Coy is helped here by the REME.

Lunch break on the prairie during Ex *Medicine Man 2:* Cpl Taylor, Cpl Fugatt and Capt Barron.

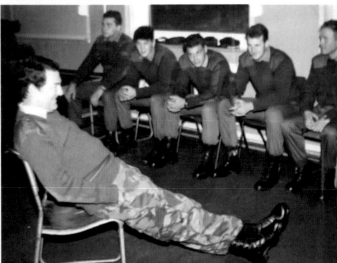

The new Colonel of the Regiment, Lt Gen Wilsey, talks with a section of the Mortar Pl: (left to right) Pte Easton, Pte Price, Pte Gooch, Pte Mackner and Pte Hubbard.

Maj Harrison and CSM Kelsall pose with B Coy on Ex *Medicine Man 2* at the British Army Training Unit Suffield (BATUS), Canada.

On Ex *Medicine Man 2* the Drums (9 Pl) had the opportunity to practise their operational skills on the Canadian prairie: (left to right) LCpl Vaastra, LCpl Hussey, Pte Moody, Pte Radmore, Pte Syms, Pte Lawry and Pte Sherratt.

the Battalion took part in Ex *Rhino Express II*, run by 6 Armoured Brigade, at Hammelburg.

In early March 1992 Lieutenant Colonel Simon Young, son of Guy Young, the first CO of the 1st Battalion, assumed command from Lieutenant Colonel Biles. Soon some 400 members of the Battalion – two reinforced companies, A and B, and a strong echelon element – were preparing to go to Canada as part of the Life Guards Battle Group. After gunnery training and testing at Bergen-Hohne ranges, thus completing conversion to the armoured infantry role, they flew to Canada in late May. With an almost brand-new fleet of *Warriors*, they soon settled down to a series of progressive fire-and-manoeuvre exercises on the huge training area. On 3rd July, just back from Canada, the 1st Battalion took part in the 6 Armoured Brigade disbandment parade, the first tangible sign that times were changing. After a hectic first year, the pace slackened slightly in the autumn although there was another spell at Soltau in October. The Battalion hosted a most enjoyable visit from 85 Old Comrades while there were opportunities for adventure training, with modest numbers getting away to far-flung places such as the Himalayas and Patagonia.

The following year was taken up almost entirely by the next tour in Northern Ireland, due to commence in early May. During January the *Warriors* were inspected before being 'put to bed'. On 1 February 1993 the Battalion's order of battle was adjusted to reflect the forthcoming commitment. The Recce Platoon was strengthened and Support Company became a rifle company once again. At this time news came through that C Company had been awarded the '*Warrior* Sword', the prize for the best

Cpl Griffiths, Cpl Holt, Cpl Pearce and Cpl Whitworth, together with their ladies, Corporals' Mess Christmas Draw, 1992.

SMI Town, now of the APTC, but formerly of the Regiment, referee of the Inter-Company Boxing Competition, announces that Pte Trim of C Coy has won the Welterweight Final against Pte Cook of B Coy.

Pte Palmer, Pte Pinsent, Pte Trick. Pte Hall, Pte Medway, Pte Shopland and Pte Grayson paddle their home-built raft across the Möhnesee during the Brigade Commander's Test Day, April 1993.

A and B Coys put together a combined Rugby Team to take on RUC Belfast at Fort Whiterock during the Northern Ireland tour in 1993: those pictured enjoying a little light refreshment before the kick-off include LCpl Hunt, Sgt Baxter, Maj Sharpe, Lt Uden, Pte Smith, Cpl Penhaligan, Sgt Bridgeman, Sgt Marland, Pte Easton, Cpl Campbell, LCpl Harvey, Pte Haines, Lt Cleave, Cpl Aston, Sgt Hale, Pte Lewis, LCpl Morris and Pte Penfold.

Manning the Broadway OP, Northern Ireland, which is equipped with all manner of electronic wizardry: (left to right) LCpl Rintoul, Cpl Conway and Pte Ackland.

Warrior live-firing in BAOR the previous year. The countdown for Ulster took a now-familiar form, briefings, specialist training and a detailed reconnaissance of the TAOR. This was also a period rich in sporting success: the 1st Battalion won the Infantry Rugby Cup, were runners-up in the BAOR Football Cup and were also runners-up in the Army Boxing, beaten once again by 1 Kings.

Belfast 1993

The Advance Party left for Belfast on 27 April 1993, with the Main Body arriving on 5 May. Northern Ireland tours had now been extended from four months to six months, reflecting the reduced intensity of operations. HQ Company and C Company (Major Barnes) were at Grosvenor Road East and North Howard Street Mill, A Company (Major Blewett) was at Ballymurphy, B Company (Major Sharpe) was at Whiterock and Echelon was based at Musgrove Park Hospital. Compared with previous tours, incidents were few and far between; nevertheless there could be no relaxation of vigilance. On 10 May A Company made an initial find that exemplified the nature of the job. A pair of surgical gloves was discovered in a coal bunker; closer examination revealed a coiled-up command wire, prompting an intense search, which in turn unearthed an IRA *Mark 12* horizontally-fired mortar, complete with mortar

The Colonel-in-Chief talks to A Coy personnel at Fort Whiterock while Maj Blewett and WO2 Braddon 56 look on expectantly.

Pte Reynolds, wearing equipment very different from that used on earlier Northern Ireland tours, is busily engaged in winning the 'hearts and minds' of the Turf Lodge community, Belfast 1993.

An impressive showing by the QM's Dept as RQMS Perrin and Sgt Greenaway man a Vehicle Check Point on Stockmans Lane in West Belfast.

Sgt Hale and Cpl Flower lead C Coy patrols from North Howard Street Mill, Belfast 1993.

LCpl Farmer and his patrol pose for a photograph in, of all unlikely places, the unloading bay.

bomb. All was quiet in B Company's area until the local elections of 19 May. As polling boxes were being collected, a device, which fortunately failed to explode, was thrown at an RUC Inspector. C Company's first 'incident' was unconnected with terrorism. A patrol saw a woman running from her house with her clothes on fire as a result of a chip pan accident. Although the woman suffered fifteen per cent burns, Private Povey managed to put the fire out with his bare hands and duly received a GOC's Commendation. It was through such actions that the Battalion maintained exceptionally good relations with the local population. Even July's Protestant marching season passed off quietly. Although everything seemed fairly low key, C Company conducted eighty-five searches and experienced five shooting incidents during those six months. The only casualty was Lance-Corporal Steve Kerslake, who was shot and wounded at Beachmount. The Colonel-in-Chief visited Belfast on 23 September 1993 and the Battalion was back in Werl by early November.

Werl

The 1st Battalion now had to get the *Warriors* out of mothballs, relearn those rusty armoured infantry skills and run training cadres, both to select future NCOs and also to teach low-level tactics to others. In March 1994 there was a last, almost nostalgic, trip to Soltau for Ex *Janners' Return*. After forty-five years Soltau was finally closing as a British Army training area. The following month there was a gunnery camp at Bergen-Hohne, part of the work-up for Ex *Medicine Man 3* in Canada. In May, as an indication of how dramatically the European military landscape had changed in just five years, the Battalion took part in Ex *Outreach* in Poland. As part of the Army's restructuring there was a more serious loss, at least from the Regimental point of view

Sgt Jessop clocks a four-man patrol in at a checkpoint during the Junior NCO's Cadre, February 1994: (left to right) Pte Shopland, Pte Stone, Pte Burt and Pte Tapscott.

– the Band was to be disbanded. The contribution made by the Regimental Band during the previous thirty-six years cannot be overstated; not only did they have a military role, as was amply demonstrated during the first Gulf War, but they helped knit the Regimental family together through their distinctive contribution. No parade, church service, Regimental boxing evening, Guest Night, Freedom march or KAPE tour would have had the same sense of occasion without their presence. Some of the Band members went to the Prince of Wales's Division Band while others joined the TA Band in Exeter. However, that was not the only major change: as part of the downsizing of BAOR, the British Army was leaving Werl, which had been a very happy single battalion station, and the 1st Battalion moved in stages to Paderborn, a much larger garrison.

By this stage of the H Jones Competition, members of 7 Pl are beginning to question what they are doing with a spare tyre strapped to their stretcher, Werl 1992.

Chapter 18

Paderborn

(including Bosnia 1995, Belize 1996 and Northern Ireland 1996/97)

1994-1998

❧

With elements of the Battalion split between Werl and Paderborn, the summer of 1994 was not the easiest period, particularly with Barker Barracks still resembling a building site. Fortunately the necessary focus was provided by Ex *Medicine Man 3* in Canada. Bearing in mind how facilities in Germany were being squeezed, the huge training area at Suffield in Alberta assumed even greater

When Fire Sp Coy is visited by the Adjt, Capt Gibb, during Ex *Medicine Man*, Capt Cavanagh shows off his helmet and matching top: Cpl Fox and Pte Ford look less than impressed.

Capt North, MTO, and WO2 Braddon 42, his MTWO, compare body armour in Canada.

Pte Foot of C Coy appears to be quite attached to the grenade clutched tightly in his right hand. What happens next?

LCpl Darmanin and Pte Philp of the Atk Pl keep a close eye on developments, with their *Milan* anti-tank missile at the ready, Bosnia 1995.

Sorting out the ammunition for the live-firing exercises on Ex *Medicine Man* can be tiring work: Capt Hartley takes a breather while RQMS Perrin wonders if everyone has got their fair share.

importance. As usual, the training was both progressive and fast-moving, culminating in battle group fire and manoeuvre. During the remainder of the year the emphasis was on inter-platoon competitions. A Company won both the inter-company Ransome Cup for football and the cross-country competition while B Company remained Champion Company with 5 Platoon winning the *Sarah Sands* march-and-shoot competition and 4 Platoon coming second in the H Jones competition. Early in 1995 there were more training cadres as a consequence of the constant demand for *Warrior* drivers and gunners, as well as junior NCOs. There was a tragedy on the latter cadre when Private Matthews was killed by a train during a night navigation exercise. There then followed an intensive period of training for the next operational commitment, Op *Grapple* in Bosnia. In March Lieutenant Colonel Jeff Cook assumed command from Lieutenant Colonel Young.

Bosnia, 1995

The *Warriors*, resplendent in their white United Nations livery, sailed from Emden, via Southampton, to Split. The 1st Battalion flew to Bosnia in late April, assuming responsibility for its duties as 'BRITBAT 1' on 4 May 1995. A Company (Major Watson) was based at Gornjï Vakuf, B

Op *Grapple*, May 1995: B Coy getting used to the nomadic life at Tomislavgrad.

Personal hygiene taken very seriously: after your kit has been washed and hung out to dry, what could be more natural than airing your feet on the front of a *Warrior*?

White-painted *Warriors*, with the lead vehicle driven by Pte Thompson, ascend the tortuous and dusty forest track up Mount Igman, the main route from Croatia into Bosnia.

A *Milan* detachment from D Coy move out of camp on a training exercise near Tomislavgrad: (left to right) LCpl Roberts, LCpl Ford and Pte Partridge.

Company (Major McFarlane) and Battalion HQ were at Vitez while C Company (Major Barnes) was at Žepče/Jelah. Liaison responsibilities, so vital with the Battalion dispersed in this way, rested with HQ Fire Support Company. During the first three weeks there was an eerie calm. The companies mounted guards and manned checkpoints and they attempted to win 'hearts and minds' by, for example, playing football and providing medical assistance. At

The 1st Battalion established its Forward Operating Base at the brick factory in Kiseljak, a small town some 30 kms north-west of Sarajevo.

the end of May relations between the Bosnian Serbs and the UN deteriorated. The Serbs attacked UN Safe Areas, the UN responded with air strikes and the Serbs reacted by taking members of the UN hostage. The 1st Battalion reconfigured to become the Bosnia-Herzegovina Command Reserve and concentrated on Vitez, pending new orders. For a week the Battalion waited while the international community wrestled with the issues. The Battalion then moved to Tomislavgrad for field-firing exercises, which were as much for demonstration purposes as they were part of a training programme. By early July the Multi-National Brigade was formed; the 1st Battalion became Task Force Alpha while the French Le Deuxième Régiment Etranger

Preparing a Range Card at an OP on Mount Igman.

Maj Harrison engages with the younger members of the population in Bosnia during the Op *Grapple* tour.

Members of 5 Pl, B Coy pose for the cameras on Mount Igman: they include (left to right) Sgt Cochrane, Pte Lister, Pte Booth, Sgt Collyer, LCpl Case, Pte Griffiths, Pte Kaster, LCpl Hanger and Cpl Jenkins.

Maj Barnes, OC C Coy, showing off his steely glare, together with an impressive, American-style selection of badges.

To the amusement of his comrade in arms (who has sensibly slung his *SA-80),* Cpl Wood only just manages to keep his footing while they carry a stretcher across a girder bridge.

Warriors from A Coy move slowly past the burnt-out mosque in Lokve on their way to Mount Igman, while the villagers carry on with their daily lives.

Have the stirring words of Kate Adie, the BBC's news correspondent – in white in the background – caused the cam cream on the faces of LCpl Beattie, Pte Kirkham and Pte Brait to run?

d'Infanterie became Task Force Bravo, leading to a lasting relationship, later formalised by a Bond of Friendship between the two Battalions.

On 23 July 1995 the 1st Battalion, in *Warriors* now repainted in their traditional black and green camouflage, escorted artillery and engineer equipment onto Mount Igman, where the Serbs had controlled the eleven-mile Mount Igman trail, the only route into, or out of, Sarajevo, for the previous three years. At long last this signified a real declaration of intent from the international community. During this period of tension Corporal Harvey of B Company won the MC, having twice extracted his *Warrior* under fire, using his weapon systems to good effect. The NATO offensive commenced on 30 August with several days of air strikes and artillery bombardments,

Capt Titley's briefing to members of the Wives' Club taking part in provocatively-named Ex *Gasalot* appears to have driven Mrs Clarke to fervent prayer, Paderborn 1996.

which eventually brought the Bosnian Serbs to the negotiating table. Throughout September the 1st Battalion was warned, briefed and then stood down for numerous operations, including Op *Cygnet 7*, the lifting of the siege around Sarajevo. By late September the Serbs at last agreed to allow free UN movement and, from then on, the Battalion's task was to guarantee safe passage for humanitarian aid coming into Sarajevo. The

dreadful living conditions and abject poverty of the local population made a lasting impression on all who participated in these operations. Having been widely praised for the job that they had done, the 1st Battalion returned to Germany in early November.

Paderborn

The programme for 1996 was subject to rapid adjustment in the light of the end of the IRA's so-called, eighteen-month 'ceasefire' in February. Earlier that month the Battalion completed field-firing at Sennelager, with A Company, B Company and a major portion of Fire Support Company preparing to go to Canada with 2 Royal Tank

After a three-mile run, candidates on the Junior NCO's Cadre concentrate hard on the written test, Paderborn 1996: (left to right) LCpl Piper, Pte Drake and Pte Mills.

Pte Stringer certainly looks the part on Ex *Airborne Janner*, adventurous training that took place after Ex *Medicine Man*, Canada, May 1996.

It wasn't all hard work as members of C Coy go trekking in the jungle of Belize: they include (left to right) Cpl Fox, LCpl Hill, LCpl Hirst and Pte Stevens.

Cpl Conway, Recce Pl, thinks very hard before putting pen to paper.

Those who didn't care to skydive after Ex *Medicine Man* could always opt to go white-water rafting on the Kananaskis River, May 1996: the happy rafters include (left to right) Sgt Edmonds, Pte Melton, Pte Sutcliffe and Pte Cornwall.

Members of C Coy practise their river crossing and raft-making skills during Ex *Native Trail*, Belize, 1996.

As a result of the decision to centralise Army bands, the 1st Battalion lost its Band: members of the 4th Battalion Band made a special trip to Paderborn to join the 1st Battalion Band for this farewell concert. Over the years the Bands have made an invaluable contribution to the Regimental family.

Regiment Battle Group in May. This time there was a new dimension to those preparations with the US Army training facilities at Grafenwohr and Hohenfels being made available for the first time; these included SIMNET, a computer-generated war game, with participants spread round an enormous hangar. Meanwhile C Company, who had nothing particularly exciting in the diary, suddenly found themselves on Ex *Nature Trail* in Belize for seven weeks, having taken the place of 1 Grenadier Guards at very short notice. After summer leave, the Battalion reorganised once again for its forthcoming Northern Ireland role as Rural Reinforcement Battalion: for example, Fire Support Company sent no less than thirty-seven soldiers to other companies and formed itself into four platoons for patrol work. Initially only one company actually went to the Province, with the others remaining at Paderborn, albeit on short notice to move.

Northern Ireland, 1996/97

On 11 December 1996 Fire Support Company was the first to deploy to Ireland. They returned in late January, having spent their time in Fermanagh. C Company succeeded them in Fermanagh, staying there until 7th April. Meanwhile B Company had deployed platoons for shorter periods. 5 Platoon joined Fire Support Company at Lisnaskea in January, to be replaced by 6 Platoon the following month. Reconstituted B Company went to Fermanagh in February, spent March in Lisburn and at the Maze Prison before being sent to East Tyrone for three weeks in April. Over the same period A Company was initially deployed in Tyrone, before guarding the Maze Prison and spending April in Fermanagh and Lisnaskea. It was a crazy merry-go-round with everyone back in Paderborn by 4 June 1997. The general conclusion was that this was

On 12 January 1998 the Bürgermeister of Paderborn, Herr Wilhelm Lüke OBE, escorted by Lt Col Watson, the new CO, and Maj Messervy, inspects a Guard of Honour as the 1st Battalion bid farewell to Paderborn.

hardly the most effective way to conduct operations. Nevertheless there were a number of noteworthy incidents that reflected extremely well on the Battalion's professionalism under trying circumstances. In December a patrol took a chance photograph of a seemingly innocent cattle truck in a farmyard, only for the same truck to be found the following day on the border, laden with explosives. On 21 March Private Lewis of C Company stumbled upon a Brazilian heavy machine-gun tripod, a home-made grenade and a quantity of ammunition. This find provoked a response from the IRA at Roselea a week later.

Paderborn

While A Company brought the 1st Battalion's tour of duty in Ulster to a close, the other companies began preparations for the central feature of the year's training, another battle group exercise in Canada. There were study days and field-firing on Bergen-Hohne ranges, tactical work-up exercises at Grafenwohr and a final session of live firing at Bergen-Hohne in mid-July. August was spent at Suffield, where the 1st Battalion demonstrated a mastery of the armoured infantry role, resulting in a Level 5 grade from the umpires, the highest that could be achieved. This was a crowning achievement for Lieutenant Colonel Cook as he handed over his responsibilities as CO to Lieutenant Colonel Jon Watson that September. From 20 September to 12 October 1997 the 1st Battalion Battle Group deployed to Poland for Ex *Ulan Eagle*, a challenging 20 Armoured Brigade/1 UK Division exercise over ground that had quite literally been 'enemy territory' less than eight years earlier. That autumn attention was focused on preparing Barker Barracks, the vehicles and equipment for handover, prior to the move to Warminster in the new year.

Chapter 19

The Wider Regimental
Family and TA

1990-1997

❦

In the immediate aftermath of the 'Options for Change' review the 1st Battalion in Germany was relatively unaffected. Although major units had been disbanded and some long-standing training areas returned to local interests, the Battalion had only been affected by an unanticipated move from Werl to Paderborn and the loss of the

At Wyvern Barracks, Exeter on 28 September 1991 the 4th Battalion received their first Colours from the Colonel-in-Chief: the Colour Party comprised (left to right) Lt Kearney, CSgt Jefferies, WO2 O'Connor, CSgt Dare and Lt Woodall.

Cadets from Devon and Dorset pause on a track during their four-day trek over the White Mountains of western Crete.

Lt Col Thornburn, CO of the 4th Battalion, with Padre Wall at Annual Camp, Stanford Training Area.

The Chairman and Secretary of the London Branch, together with the President and Secretary of The Regimental Association at the Regiment's plot at the Field of Remembrance, Westminster Abbey, on 11 November 1993: (left to right) Lt Col Roberts, Mr Bloomfield, Gen Wilsey and Mrs May Glover.

The Colonel-in-Chief visits the 4th Battalion during its Annual Camp on Salisbury Plain: the group includes Cpl Nicholls and Pte Loader.

Regimental Band. This relatively charmed life was a tribute to the new Colonel of the Regiment, Lieutenant General John Wilsey, who had succeeded Major General Colin Shortis in May 1990. At that time the Regiment, with one regular and one TA battalion, coupled with a strong regional recruiting base, faced the future with justifiable confidence. This was misplaced. Within months it was announced that no less than seventeen infantry battalions were to be disbanded over the next few years. Regimentally, we had our backs to the wall and, with the help of RHQ, the Colonel of the Regiment prepared his arguments: the Regiment had a proven ability to recruit and retain both officers and soldiers, there were very strong links with both counties, the Regiment had already suffered an earlier amalgamation, there were distinct benefits in having paired regular and TA battalions, the Regiment's proud record of service and, lastly, the seniority of the Regiment, deriving from the 11th Foot. This time the Regiment did survive but, according to General Wilsey, it would not have done so 'without the Herculean efforts of a very large number of people'.

The long and dedicated service of Mr and Mrs Gigg typifies that of many members of the Regimental family: having served as a WO2 in the Regiment, he later joined the TA and served as Secretary of the *Semper Fidelis Dinner Club* for 15 years; a daughter of D/Maj Godfrey, 1 Devon, Mrs Gigg ran the Kindergarten for many years and made an invaluable contribution to the Wives' Club.

In fact the Regiment not only survived but the 4th Battalion was actually strengthened as D Company, 1 Wessex at Poole became D Company, 4 D and D, rebadging in June 1992. On 28 September 1991 the 4th Battalion was presented with Colours by the Colonel-in-Chief and, by late 1992, it was close to establishment. They were equipped with the *SA80* assault rifle and light support weapon and, by April 1993,

Devon ACF mark WO1 Langman's retirement at the Last Post Ceremony at the Menin Gate, Ypres 1993: (left to right) Cdt RSM Aldgate, WO1 Langman, Col Reason, ACF County Commandant, and Cdt RSM Simpson.

Maj Mellin of Devon ACF coaches Cadet SSgt France of Braunton, North Devon on the battle shooting range at Otterburn in 1994. Having done National Service with the Australian Army, Maj Mellin returned to England and did a further spell of National Service with 1 Devon. He then signed up for a regular engagement, joined the 1st Battalion after amalgamation and reached the rank of Sergeant before transferring to the SASC. After a distinguished career in the SASC, Maj Mellin returned to Devon, helping Devon ACF to win many shooting competitions.

Members of the 4th Battalion on an adventurous training exercise in the Troodos Mountains, Cyprus: (left to right) LCpl Hill, LCpl Sparks, Cpl Jellard and Pte Wellaway.

CSgt Brown and CSgt Strickland, Echelon, C Coy, 4 D and D serve up a meal on Salisbury Plain: Maj Faussett and Cpl Arman (right) appear less than convinced of its nourishing qualities.

The Regimental Colours of both the 1st Battalion and the 4th Battalion appear together – an historic first – during the parade at which the Regiment was granted the Freedom of Sherborne on 28 May 1994: front row (left to right) Lt Maynard, WO2 Williams, RQMS Chivers.

The Presentation and Display Team manned by HQ Coy of the 4th Battalion won the award for the Best Display at the Mid-Devon Show, summer 1994: those present include Sgt Loman, Sgt Jeffrey, Capt Jeapes, Cpl Williams and LCpl Jeffery.

had become a light role TA infantry battalion. Following the demise of the Regimental Band, the Volunteer Band assumed a far greater importance. During the summers of 1994 and 1995 there were a succession of parades to commemorate the momentous events of the liberation of Europe from Nazi domination fifty years earlier – the Volunteer Band played an important part at all of them.

Although RHQ had escaped 'Options for Change' unscathed, there was now an urgent requirement to establish a single Regimental Museum. It was agreed that The Military Museum of Devon and Dorset would be in the Keep at Dorchester. The chairman of the Regimental Museum project was Major General Shortis and, in April 1993, the Colonel of the Regiment launched a Regimental Appeal to pay for the

Led by Sgt Dicker, a heavily-laden patrol from D Coy, 4 D and D moves tactically through the woods during a battalion exercise at Bovington.

The Colonel-in-Chief presents LCpl Read with his Long Service and Good Conduct medal at The Keep Military Museum of Devon and Dorset, Dorchester, 5 September 1996: after being wounded while serving with the 1st Battalion in Northern Ireland, LCpl Read was posted to the Museum, where he made a major contribution.

refurbishment of the Keep, which was looking extremely 'tired'. In the event a total of £180,000 was raised from the Regimental Appeal and The Military Museum of Devon and Dorset was formally opened by HRH The Duke of Kent on 27 May 1994. At the same time the Colonel-in-Chief launched the Public Appeal for Phase 2 Development, orchestrated by General Sir John Archer. The total sum raised by both appeals was £485,000 and the result is a Regimental Museum that stands comparison with any in the country.

At the end of his Colonelcy on 31 December 1997, General Sir John Wilsey said: 'I want to thank RHQ on my own behalf, and on behalf of the whole Regiment, for the key part they play at the very centre of the Regiment. Seldom does one read in these pages [of the *Regimental Journal*] about the work of those at RHQ. But that tiny dedicated staff, headed up by Colin Pape, is immersed in every aspect of Regimental life. It is through RHQ that we get our officers; RHQ co-ordinate our soldier recruiting effort, they run our outstanding Regimental museum and out-stations, they are at the very centre of our Regimental Association and are the link with the Devon and Dorset

ACF and fourteen CCFs. They are the interface with our twelve Freedom Cities and Towns. In short, they fly the flag for the Regiment outstandingly well in every corner of the counties, and provide our formal link to the Colonel-in-Chief and Prince of Wales's Division HQ. We all owe them a great deal of gratitude, and as my last act as Colonel, I pay my own tribute to them through the pages of this fine *Journal* which – yet another task – the Regimental Secretary himself edits.'

The Keep Military Museum of Devon and Dorset: in the mid-1990s £485,000 was raised by the Museum Appeal. The money was spent on the refurbishment of the building and the modernising of the extensive displays.

Chapter 20

Warminster
1998-2000

❦

*D*uring the previous seven years the 1st Battalion had been at the cutting edge of the British Army, serving in the armoured infantry role. At Warminster the skills honed in Germany, on the prairies of Canada and in Bosnia would now be used in training other British Army units as the Combined Arms Tactics Centre Battle Group (CATC BG). The 1st Battalion assumed responsibility for CATC BG on 16 February 1998. Apart from the Battalion, the Battle Group comprised a squadron of tanks, a recce troop, a Royal Engineer close support troop and a large REME Light Aid Detachment. CATC BG supported the various Warminster-based courses, which ran in three-month cycles, by providing both friendly and enemy forces for the student officers. 'Friendly forces' comprised A Company (Major House), equipped with the old *AFV 432*; C Company (Major Uden), equipped with *Warrior*, together with elements of D (Support) Company (Major Gibb). 'Enemy forces' were represented by B Company (Major Messervy), who were equipped with disguised *AFV 432s* and wore distinguishing desert combats. During the next two years the Battalion would become extremely familiar with exercises such as *Iron Maiden*, *Phantom Bugle* and *Iron Fist*. Perhaps the most demanding task was putting visiting units through TESEXs (Tactical Engagement Systems Exercises), for which every soldier, vehicle and weapon was fitted with

Cpl Kent of the Recce Pl at Yuma, Arizona, where he carried out trials on the 0.338 long-range large calibre rifle on behalf of the Infantry Trials and Development Unit: fortunately he wasn't expected to carry it both there and back!

The Mayor of Blandford is briefed on the intricacies of *Milan* at the County Representatives' Day, 18 June 1998: Maj Sharpe and Don Mildenhall, formerly of *Pullman's Weekly*, a loyal Regimental supporter over many years, can be seen in the background.

The Wild Bunch, Warminster 1998: Cpl Breslan and his section explore common ground with Michaela Strachan, presenter of BBC wild-life programmes such as *The Really Wild Guide* and *The Animal Zone*.

The Colonel-in-Chief visited the 1st Battalion at Warminster on 23 March 1999: (left to right) Lt Col Watson, CO, the Colonel-in-Chief, Maj Storrie, OC C Coy.

The JNCO's Cadre steeplechase competition, Warminster 1999: Cpl Harvey encourages a tiring section, which includes Pte Bibbick and Pte Poulton.

laser transmitters/receivers. The opposing forces then engaged one another, using the resulting data to improve their understanding and employment of tactical doctrine. During the 1st Battalion's time at Warminster the Firepower Demonstration was resited from the edge to the centre of Salisbury Plain, involving a complete redesign of this very public 'performance'. The role at Warminster was extremely high profile, with a seemingly never-ending stream of visitors, both from the UK and also from overseas.

A particular advantage of the Warminster posting was the relative predictability of the diary: everyone knew months – if not years – in advance what

While stationed at Warminster the 1st Battalion was extremely well placed to strengthen West Country links: D (Sp) Coy at the Devon County Show, May 1999 (left to right) LCpl Pike, LCpl Boot, LCpl Clark and Capt Bryant.

would be happening. As must now be apparent to the reader, that is a luxury seldom enjoyed by an infantry battalion in the British Army! This was relevant in that, after almost seven years in Germany, there was a great deal of catching-up to be done in the West Country. On 9 May 1998 Regimental Day was held in Torbay, with a march that marked the 25th Anniversary of the granting of the Freedom of the Borough to the Regiment. For the first time there was a real opportunity to establish a close relationship between the 1st and 4th Battalions. For example, there was a joint visit to the Bois des Buttes Memorial that May and a meeting of the *Semper Fidelis Dinner Club* at Babbacombe on 24 October 1998. Sadly it was announced in early 1999 that the short life of the 4th Battalion was coming to an end. On 5 June 1999 the Battalion

"What do we do if the balloon goes up?" LCpl Milton, Capt Finnamore and Pte Crane at the Devon County Show in May 1999.

In the assembly area for Ex *Phantom Bugle*, held on Salisbury Plain in early October 1999, can be seen an impressive variety of military hardware, including *Scimitars, Warriors* and a Combat Engineer Tractor.

Maj Edkins uses sign language to explain to Baroness Symons, Minister of State for Defence Procurement, how defence expenditure can be 'chopped', Warminster, 5 December 1999.

Briefing during Ex *Phantom Bugle*, Salisbury Plain, October 1999: (left to right) LCpl Hughes, Pte Harker and Pte Bloxham.

The Colours of the 1st Battalion and the 4th Battalion were on parade together when the Regiment exercised the Freedom of Torquay on 9 May 1998: the 1st Battalion Colour Party comprised Lt Dunlop, Lt Murray, WO2 Hilton, CSgt Smith and CSgt Day; the 4th Battalion Colour Party comprised WO2 Jeffries, CSgt Longman and CSgt Watmore.

Sgt Murch leads No 1 Guard during the Freedom Parade, Torquay, 9 May 1998.

paraded for the last time at the Regimental Day in Exeter before disbanding on 30 June. The good news was that C and E Companies became part of the new Rifle Volunteers: at the Freedom March through Bridport on 25 September 1998 guards from both these companies marched proudly alongside those from the 1st Battalion.

Two members of the Regiment deserve mention for their sporting achievements. Major Peter Underhill, Combined Services Sportsman of the Year in 1999, was Captain of the Army Combat Shooting Team while Lance-Corporal Tom Clemens, the 20 km Biathlon Army Champion, later became the National Champion. Adventurous training has always played an important role and the Regiment acquired its own adventurous training centre when the lease of Ligger House in Cornwall was purchased in 1999. A particularly high profile task throughout the tour of duty in Warminster was The Combined Arms Firepower and Manoeuvre Demonstration (CAFMD). Brigadier David Shaw saw the Battalion's final performance: 'Manoeuvre is what shows the real professionals at work and our 1st Battalion was quite magnificent ... I saw a professional display of military competence, (of) weapon systems adroitly handled and with great confidence ... The Army is highly respected in this country and the 1st Battalion has contributed a great deal to that reputation.'

The Army helped a member of the Regiment, LCpl Clemens, to fulfil his sporting potential: a former Army and National 20 kilometre Biathlon Champion, British World Cup Team Member 1998/99, LCpl Clemens represented Great Britain at the 2005 Winter Olympics.

The *GPMG* produces plenty of cordite smoke when fired in the SF role: (left to right) Pte Wall, Pte Quinn, Pte Hayes, Pte Evans and Pte Mackintosh.

If only adventurous training were always as relaxing as this: LCpl Vaastra, LCpl Pooley and Sgt Edwards sailing in the English Channel.

The 1st Battalion Football Team, Warminster 1998: back row (left to right) Cpl Hetherington, Cpl Elliott, Pte Bartlett, LCpl Burt, LCpl Pincombe, Pte Sharrock, Sgt Knight, Cpl Clift; front row (left to right) Pte Light, Pte Cook, WO2 Symns (Coach), CSgt Campbell (Captain), Pte Witt, Pte Austin.

LCpl Quick (left) of the Aslt Pnrs at the General Salute during the Freedom Parade in Torquay on 9 May 1998.

Chapter 21

Hounslow

(including Armagh 2000/01
and Belize 2001)

2000-2002

In mid-March 2000 the 1st Battalion moved some ninety miles east, to Cavalry Barracks in Hounslow. Initially there were some long faces: Cavalry Barracks had been condemned, pigeons were nesting in the eaves of the Officers' Mess and there was even official recognition of the situation in that accommodation charges were, quite exceptionally, waived. Coincident with the move to Hounslow, there was a change of command, as Lieutenant Colonel Watson handed over to Lieutenant Colonel Richard Toomey. There was slight puzzlement concerning the Battalion's task – 'light role with jungle focus' – which sounded suspiciously Gilbert and Sullivan! Actually it

When the Regiment was granted the Freedom of Shaftesbury, the Freedom Scroll, carried by Pte Willis, was paraded through the streets of the town, escorted by the Aslt Pnrs, with the 1st Battalion marching behind, 15 April 2000: Lt Col Toomey, the new CO, Maj Bryant, OC B Coy, and CSgt Sims also appear in this view.

During the 1st Battalion's time at Hounslow, Public Duties were never very far away. These soldiers are waiting at the barracks in Windsor prior to the mounting of the Windsor Castle Guard: the group includes Sgt Newcombe, LCpl Caple, Cpl Hawkins, LCpl Hill, Pte Crighton, LCpl Cole, Pte Lane, Pte Betuschi, Pte Hill and Pte Cleaver.

A 'stick' from 5 Pl, B Coy, including Pte Giddings and LCpl McKinley, returns safely to Bessbrook Mill by *Lynx*, South Armagh, 2001.

Members of 6 Pl – callsign 30B – at location G40, one of the so-called 'Golf Towers', South Armagh, 2001: back row (left to right) LCpl Bell, Cpl Lunness, Sgt Farmer, LCpl Read, Pte Walker, Pte Lamont, Pte McCuaig; front row (left to right) Pte Jeans, Pte March, Pte Daniel, Pte Jones, Pte Hills, Pte Ticehurst.

Pte Atkins and Pte Manns, both of A Coy, inside the base at Crossmaglen, November 2001.

was an elaborate smokescreen: the main task was Public Duties. The first few months at Hounslow were dominated by parades. On 15 April 2000 the Regiment received the Freedom of Shaftesbury. B Company had already started preparing for Public Duties and provided the Windsor Castle Guard for the whole of May. On 3 June the Battalion was central to the success of the Regimental Day, which took place that year at Exeter. Preparations for the forthcoming tour in Armagh then became the priority. After a briefing in early June, the Battalion went to the ranges at Hythe and Lydd and then on to Stanford, where the training concluded with the traditional *Sarah Sands* march-and-shoot. The commitment was for three large rifle companies and, with the 1st Battalion now ninety under strength, some restructuring became necessary: C Company and Fire Support Company were both temporarily disbanded and No 3 Company, Welsh Guards came under command.

Armagh, 2000/01

After a spell of summer leave, the Battalion was established in Armagh by 15 September: Battalion HQ at Bessbrook; A Company (Major Bromham) at Crossmaglen, with elements of C Company under command at Newtonhamilton; B Company (Major Beattie) at Forkhill and No 3 Company, Welsh Guards (Major Lloyd), with a platoon from C Company and the Recce Platoon, at Bessbrook. While the dispositions were similar to those of the 1972 tour, the overall Ulster situation had recently been transformed by the 'Good Friday Agreement'. Although this six-month tour generated few memorable 'incidents', it nevertheless demanded the levels of professionalism and self-discipline that would convince the IRA that the Agreement really had to be made to work. Two other differences were that the Army was very much subsidiary to, and working in support of, the Police Service of Northern Ireland

B Coy Windsor Castle Guard, May 2000: LCpl Cook posting Pte Cole, who is relieving Pte Moore, at the Sentry Box outside the Guardroom.

The Colonel-in-Chief presented new Colours to the 1st Battalion at Wyvern Barracks, Exeter on 28 July 2000: RSM Smith hands the old Colours to the Ensigns, Lt Bryan (Queen's Colour) and Lt Jellard (Regimental Colour).

On 28 July 2000 the 1st Battalion's new Colours were blessed by the Venerable John Blackburn, Chaplain General to the Forces: facing him are Maj Field, Lt Richards and Lt Col Toomey.

to counter the threat from Republican dissidents. Meanwhile 'foot and mouth' restrictions applied just as much in rural Northern Ireland as they did elsewhere in the UK, thus restricting patrolling activity to a minimum in early 2001. There was also a slight drama over Christmas when heavy snowfalls briefly threatened the morale-boosting 'R and R' changeover. Distinguished visitors included both the Colonel-in-Chief and the Colonel of the Regiment and also that stalwart Regimental supporter, Don Mildenhall, who had been supplying hard-hitting 'copy' to West Country newspapers for more than thirty years. At the end of the tour both Lieutenant Colonel Toomey and WO2 House received the Queen's Commendation for Valuable Service.

Hounslow

The 1st Battalion returned to Hounslow on 18 March 2001 and, after a spell of well-earned leave, it was back to the pace-stick and the barrack square. The 'Major-General's Inspection' took place at the end of May, with the entire Battalion on parade in No. 1 Dress; the 1st Battalion was congratulated on its 'outstanding turnout'. Following the Regimental Day at Weymouth on 2 June, there was only a succession of guard duties to look forward to: the Queen's Guard at Buckingham Palace, the Windsor Guard and the State Opening of Parliament. Free weekends became something of a novelty. For the State Opening of Parliament both the Commanding Officer and the Ops Officer (Captain Gidlow-Jackson) were required to be mounted and therefore had to attend a 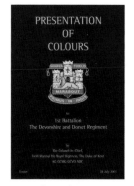 'crash course' with the Household Cavalry. The result of these experiences was that the 1st Battalion could not possibly have been better prepared for the parade at Wyvern Barracks, Exeter on 28 July 2001 at which the Colonel-in-Chief presented a new stand of Colours.

The Colonel-in-Chief and Lt Col Toomey talk to members of Le Deuxième Régiment Etranger D'Infanterie, helping to cement the Bond of Friendship established when the two Regiments were part of the same Rapid Reaction Force on Op *Hermine* in Bosnia in 1995.

Ex *Suman Warrior* is an annual exercise between nations of the Five Power Defence Arrangement (FPDA): the United Kingdom, Singapore, Malaysia, Australia and New Zealand. In October 2001 the exercise was hosted by the Australian Army and took place in Brisbane, where these officers were heading: (left to right) Maj Uden, Maj Bennett, Lt Col Toomey, Capt Woodiwiss, Capt Kelsall and Maj Beattie.

The 1st Battalion Shooting Team, trained by Maj Underhill, pose with a splendid selection of silverware after the London District Skill-at-Arms Meeting in 2000: they include, (left to right) Lt Ford, Pte Hughes, LCpl Swabey, Maj Underhill, LCpl Conner, Cpl Mason, Cpl Bennett and Pte Harrington.

C Coy members waste no time in getting stuck into the chicken while on Ex *Panther Cub* in Belize, October 2001: (left to right) Pte Tuinaro, Pte George and Pte Connicutt.

After summer leave, which had to be staggered since there was no break from Public Duties, the Battalion went to Belize on exercise. B and C Companies flew out on 11 September 2001, a date now forever branded on human consciousness: as a result of security alerts the advance party was stranded at Dulles for eight days while the main body was stuck at Gander for four days. Meanwhile A Company took part in a moment of history as the American National Anthem was played at the Changing of the Guard outside Buckingham Palace and a two-minute silence was observed for the victims of the terrorist attacks on the United States. After their delayed start, the first two companies enjoyed a worthwhile spell of training, before they were replaced by A and D Companies. This time nature intervened in the form of Hurricane *Iris* and, for the first few days, humanitarian relief was the first priority. Those who didn't go to Belize, principally Battalion HQ and the Recce Platoon, flew to Brisbane in Australia and joined similar contingents from Australia, New Zealand, Malaysia and Singapore on Ex *Suman Warrior*. By 1st December Public Duties were over and training had begun for the next posting, which was back to Ballykinler. There was, however, one last, poignant public duty to perform. HM The Queen Mother died on 30 March 2002. The Battalion's move to Ballykinler was delayed, men were recalled from leave, 'Blues' were unexpectedly drawn out once again from the stores, new drill moves were mastered and the Battalion was immensely proud to be on parade on 9 April 2002 for the State Funeral.

On 1 June 2002 the Regiment was granted the Freedom of Exmouth: the 1st Battalion Colour Party (left to right) Lt White (Queen's Colour), CSgt Lamble, WO2 Edmonds, CSgt Harvey, Lt Leatherdale (Regimental Colour).

Hurricane *Iris* struck Belize just as B Coy completed their basic jungle training: (left to right) Cpl Hetherington, LCpl Hasker, Sgt Brody and Pte Smith take a break during the relief operation to clear up the damage, some of which can be seen below.

Chapter 22

Return to Ballykinler

2002-2004

*Al*though the Battalion had returned to Ballykinler, no more than twenty of its members had experience of the tour that ended some seventeen years earlier. A great deal had changed: 'Snatch' and 'Tavern' vehicles had replaced the old *Makralon*-armoured *Land Rovers*, vehicle communications were now secure and even a Quartermaster naturally sparing in his praise was moved to describe Abercorn Barracks as 'fantastic'. The Battalion acted as 3 Brigade's reserve, with the result that two companies were routinely committed, a third was on guard at Ballykinler, the fourth on leave while the Close Observation Platoon (COP) was heavily committed in South Armagh. In May 2002 both HQ and B Companies were involved in the Junior Orange Lodge march at Portadown, while A and C Companies were temporarily deployed in the Short Strand area of Belfast. In addition to these public

Snap Vehicle Check Point in Northern Ireland: (left to right) Pte Crabbe, Pte White, Pte Edmunds and Pte Duffy.

order activities, there was the unceasing requirement to support the Police Service in County Down and, right at the start of the tour, there were follow-ups to pipe bomb attacks on the stations at Ardnaglass and Downpatrick. In mid-year Lieutenant Colonel Sandy Storrie assumed command from Lieutenant Colonel Toomey and was soon faced with the challenge of the 14 July Protestant march at Drumcree, which had in recent years become something of a flashpoint. 3 Brigade decided that an overwhelming military presence was the answer and the 1st Battalion spent several days quietly preparing barriers and talking to local people on both sides of the sectarian divide, with the result that the march passed off very quietly.

LCpl Bray shows Henry Jones, grandson of Lt Col H Jones, the trophy named after his grandfather.

Ex *Snow Hole Finn:* Lt Luard, Cpl Eastwood, Pte Maunder and Pte Watts 39 make themselves comfortable in a snow hole.

The 1st Battalion Water Polo Team, Ballykinler, winners of the 3 Bde Water Polo Competition: they include, back row (left to right) Cpl Morley, Sgt Carne, Sgt French; front row (left to right) Pte Farley, Cpl Darmanin, Capt Gillespie, Pte Jarman, Capt Jellard.

Lt Col Storrie takes rather naturally to the part of a 'Wurzel' as he waits for his turn on the stage!

Ex *Snow Hole Finn* was a three-week, ski touring, adventurous training trip across the Hardangervidda Glacier in central Norway in March/April 2003.

One consequence of the never-ending round of Public Duties was that the Battalion came under severe manning pressures. Perhaps the most notable achievement during the two years spent at Ballykinler was the way in which this situation was tackled through a combination of retention and recruiting. In the early autumn of 2002 there were only 437 Devon and Dorset soldiers in the Battalion. Two years later the numbers had risen to 526, thus eliminating the under-manning against a light role establishment. Another key focus was the training of junior NCOs, which had also suffered at Hounslow. At the start of the Ballykinler tour there were only five School of Infantry-trained junior NCOs in the Battalion, excluding those serving with the COP; when the 1st Battalion left Ballykinler there were seven or eight in each company. While undergoing refresher training at Kirkcudbright in Scotland, Lance-Corporal Read and Lance-Corporal Hughes were killed in a road traffic accident. An interesting sign of changed times was that the Battalion provided most of the members of the British Army's Gaelic football team that played in Dublin, a visit that would have been inconceivable just a

In full voice at the 1st Battalion Christmas Carol Service, Ballykinler: (left to right) CSgt Flower, CSgt Brown, CSM Campbell, Sgt Crane and Sgt Wyatt.

Capt Cummings REME, Capt Maynard and Maj Steptoe dressed in festive gear for the Christmas 'Fun Run': a couple of them seem to be suffering from over-indulgence!

B Coy shortly after the start of the H Jones Competition 2003: Maj Jones, OC, CSM Hunt, Lt Wilson, Sgt Wyatt, Lt Sheppard, Sgt French, Cpl Cornwell.

On his first visit to the 1st Battalion after being appointed Colonel of the Regiment, Lt Gen Delves speaks to Maj Cleave, Sgt Wyatt, Lt Sheppard and other members of A Coy, June 2003.

Be prepared! WO2 Lamble points out for the camera's benefit the (unused) Casualty Evacuation Point that A Coy had prepared for the Drumcree March in 2003.

1st Battalion wives looking slightly dishevelled but distinctly relieved to be back in camp after taking part in Ex *Pretty Woman*, a 24-hour field training exercise.

The Fijian contingent has made an important contribution to the life and culture of the 1st Battalion: as part of the Fijian National Day celebrations, these soldiers are making preparations for the 'Kava Ceremony' by pounding the roots of the pepper tree into a fine powder, before mixing the result with water, Ballykinler, October 2004: they include (left to right) Pte Uludole, Pte Iranatora, Pte Tuinaro, Pte Ratukaloy and Pte Jorgensen.

few years earlier. In the autumn of 2003 the Battalion filled four of the top five placings in the 3 Brigade march-and-shoot competition.

The final months in Ballykinler were very busy. After a recruiting trip to the counties, A Company went on operations in South Armagh, B Company went on Ex *Janners' Dart,* followed by a particularly chilly visit to Galloway while C Company found two IEDs close to Ballykinler and, as a result, Corporal Borlace received a GOC's Commendation. Corporal Thomas received a Queen's Commendation for Bravery for his skill and dedication during a COP operation. In conclusion, despite the complications of drawdown and restructuring, the 1st Battalion provided reliable and professional support for the Police Service of Northern Ireland, without in any way conflicting with the policy of 'police primacy'.

Participants on Ex *Northern Solent* sailing off Portland in the summer of 2003: (rear) Pte Lake, Pte Libby, Pte Leach; (front) Pte Cowley, Lt Steevenson.

On 22 July 2003 there were challenges, fun and frivolity galore when the 1st Battalion celebrated Salamanca Day. The C Coy Chariot Race team enters fully into the spirit of things: (left to right) Pte Hall, Pte Roberts, Cpl Neale, Pte Keeley and Pte Lamont.

What happens when the firemen go on strike? Call in the Army! Members of the Atk Pl – including CSgt Penhaligan, Pte Neil, Pte Bower, Cpl Stanton, Pte Stringer, Pte Howitt, Pte Devine, Pte Harper, Pte Heywood, Pte McClean and Pte Andre – are ready to deploy at short notice from Bessbrook Mill on Op *Fresco*.

Chapter 23

The Wider Regimental Family and TA

(including Afghanistan 2004, Iraq 2006 and Afghanistan 2006/07)

1998-2007

At the beginning of 1998 Major General Bryan Dutton succeeded General Sir John Wilsey as Colonel of the Regiment. The election of a Labour Government the previous May introduced uncertainty and a Strategic Defence Review (SDR) was announced in the middle of the year. It soon became apparent that, while the Regular Army might even be slightly strengthened, TA manning would be reduced by some 40,000. By the end of the year it also became clear that the 4th Battalion would be superseded by The Rifle Volunteers, which would recruit across the whole of the South West. HQ and E Companies would remain at Exeter with a platoon at Plymouth, while C Company would remain at Dorchester with a platoon at Poole. However, the Volunteer Band escaped unscathed and the first Commanding Officer of the Rifle Volunteers was a Devon and Dorset, Lieutenant Colonel David Harrison. Under the Reserve Forces Act, The Rifle Volunteers were required to provide companies or individuals in direct support of the Regular Army on a voluntary or compulsory basis: twenty-four Rifle Volunteers were serving with an under-strength

On 29 May 1988 Maj Gen Dutton, Colonel of the Regiment, presented Lt Col Roberts – accompanied here by his wife Yvonne – with a leaving gift to mark his retirement as Assistant Regimental Secretary, after many years of unstinting devotion to the Regimental cause.

For many years Maj Cullen (left) and his wife Sandy (right) hosted the Regimental Golf Competition, the proceeds from which were given to the Keep Military Museum: Mr Andronik receives his prize, Maj Reid rechecks his scorecard in disbelief while Lt Col Jury waits somewhat hopefully in the wings.

Members of C Coy, 4 D and D clear a trench during Ex *Wyvern Tail* on Salisbury Plain.

On 2 June 2001 the Regiment's Chelsea Pensioners attended the Regimental Day at Weymouth: (left to right) In-pensioners Evans, Lord, Jeffery and Rogers.

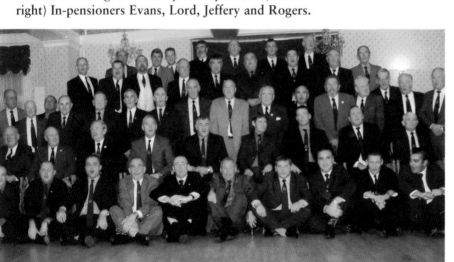

On 12 November 2000 Lord Cranborne, Honorary Colonel the 4th Battalion, officially ope the newly-refurbished E Coy li at Wyvern Barracks, Exeter.

The *Semper Fidelis Dinner Cl* (SFDC) held their 2003 Dinner at the Savoy Hotel in Bournemouth. Membership of the SFDC is open to past and present members of the Warra Officers' and Sergeants' Messe of the Regiment.

52 members of the Rifle Volunteers deployed to Afghanistan on Op *Fingal,* 6 October 2003 – 11 May 2004: Cpl Dwyer and his patrol from E Coy are offered tea and sweets by the local militia. Unfortunately relations with the local population were not always so friendly: in Kabul on 28 January 2004 a suicide bomber killed Pte Kitulagoda of E Coy and seriously injured CSgt Smith, LCpl Hart and LCpl Jones.

1st Battalion in Armagh at the end of 2000. The new Battalion was also required to assist local authorities in the event of regional emergencies and, in early 2001, provided assistance to MAFF and DEFRA during the 'foot and mouth' outbreak. The pace of TA life quickened sharply. There were exercises in Ukraine in 2001 and in Cyprus two years later. Preparing The Rifle Volunteers for FTRS (full time regular service) was vital and the support and understanding of employers essential.

Having successfully steered the Regiment through the Labour Government's SDR, Major General Dutton handed over his responsibilities as Colonel of the Regiment to Lieutenant General Sir Cedric Delves at the end of 2002. Following the refurbishment, The Military Museum of Devon and Dorset was on a very sound footing with a determined Curator, former RSM and QM, Major

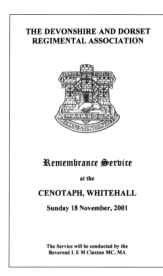

THE DEVONSHIRE AND DORSET
REGIMENTAL ASSOCIATION

Remembrance Service

at the

CENOTAPH, WHITEHALL

Sunday 18 November, 2001

The Service will be conducted by the
Reverend L E M Claxton MC, MA

Len Brown. When he died in January 1999, he was followed, in quick succession, by two retired Royal Engineer officers: first Lt Col Parmley and then Lt Col Leonard. This period saw a succession of innovative exhibitions, the opening of the Crownhill Gallery in Plymouth, the negotiation of a new 50-year lease and the separation of the Museum as a charity, with its own set of trustees.

Members of 1 Dorset who served together in Minden in the period leading up to amalgamation have formed a strong bond over the years: they have just received a new standard (left to right) Mr Gollop, Mr Moore, Rev Miller, Rev Hunham and Mr Spearman.

Members of C Coy, Devon ACF, many of whom had never played hockey before, put together a team to represent the South West Region at the ACF National Hockey Championships on 12 July 2000, eventually losing in the final to the home team: back row (left to right) Cdt Yates, Sgt Joce, Sgt Turner, Cdt Walter, Cdt Smith, Cdt Edmonds, Sgt Boyles; front row (left to right) LCpl Lucas, Cdt Gent, LCpl Lochead, Cdt Reddy, Cdt Morris; (lying) RSM Morgan.

Capt Fulford-Dobson, Lord-Lieutenant of Dorset, presents the Certificate of Appointment as the Lord-Lieutenant's Cadet to Cadet Sgt Harrison.

On the evening of 2 May 2005, before the Regimental Day in Plymouth, the Regimental Band gave a concert to celebrate the 60th Anniversary of the end of the Second World War. As can be seen, it had a 'Last Night of the Proms' atmosphere: the Colonel of the Regiment and Lady Delves are second and third from right in the front row of the balcony.

Flanked by the Standard Bearers, Messrs King and Flood, Mr Warwick, formerly of 12 Devon, popularly known as the 'Swede Bashers', proudly presents the Colonel of the Regiment, with a candle-lit swede during their annual dinner at the Devon Motel, Exeter, October 2005.

Rifle Volunteers in Iraq and Afghanistan

By early 2004 no less than 55 members of The Rifle Volunteers were taking part in Op *Fingal* in Afghanistan, a further 55 were on stand-by for Op *Telic* in Iraq and 26 others were on FTRS, bolstering an over-stretched Regular Army. These commitments were very real: Private 'Kit' Kitulagoda of The Rifle Volunteers was killed on active service in Afghanistan on 28 January 2004 while five other members of The Rifle Volunteers were wounded. In April 2004 eighty members of The Rifle Volunteers – including a number from the Devon-and Dorset-based companies – were mobilised to take part in operations in Basra as part of the 1 Cheshire Battle Group, remaining in Iraq until November. This was a very considerable commitment for 'part-time' soldiers: having taken account of pre-tour training and post-tour leave, they spent no less than ten months away from their civilian jobs. While the Ministry of Defence was naturally anxious to remove some of the  pressure on loyal volunteers and their employers, that did not deter many of the former from putting their names forward for duty once again almost as soon as they arrived home. The tour coincided with increasing tension in Basra and there were frequent contacts with insurgents, in one of which CSgt Smith was wounded. As a result of this tour Sgt Poole-Reeves was mentioned in despatches while there were GOC's Commendations for Pte Gavin and Sgt Pinnell.

In mid-2006 the Devon and Dorset TA companies provided many of the volunteers for Peninsular Company, which was mobilised for preliminary training that July before proceeding to Helmand Province, Afghanistan with 3 Commando Brigade in October.

While on Op *Fingal*, LCpl Pond relies on local transport in attempting to flee his youthful Afghani pursuers.

A patrol from the Rifle Volunteers shortly after a 'contact' with insurgents, Op *Telic*, Iraq, 2004: they include, back row (left to right) Pte Gavin, LCpl Forde, Pte Lagrenade; front row (left to right) Cpl Climber, Lt Sherwood.

A patrol from the Rifle Volunteers poses in Iraq while serving on Op *Telic*, Iraq, 2004: (standing) Sgt Pinnell, Pte Lagrenade, Sgt Poole-Reeves, Lt Sparkes, Lt Sherwood, Pte Wheelan, Sgt Peart; (seated) LCpl Visick, Pte King, LCpl Reid, Pte Rowe, Pte Morris, Pte Ziya, Pte Hammond.

The Rifle Volunteers carried out local security patrols from Camp Bastion: although lightly armoured, the *Land Rovers* packed a punch with their .50 *Browning* heavy machine guns.

Helicopter support in a vast open desert as the Rifle Volunteers deployed to Afghanistan as part of BRITFOR on Op *Herrick*, 2006/07: they include LCpl Steel, Cpl Tucker, Pte Murphy, LCpl Luscombe, Pte Proctor, LCpl Kerley and LCpl John.

Members of the Rifle Volunteers admiring the new *Apache* attack helicopter, Afghanistan: LCpl Steel, LCpl John, Pte Proctor, Pte Murphy, Cpl Tucker, LCpl Kerley and Pte Luscombe.

The six-strong Dorset ACF *Ten Tors Challenge* team, who successfully completed the demanding 45-mile course: (left to right) A Berry, M Evans, J Walker, J Thompson, D Nimmo and M Alger. The distance attempted depends on the age of the participants.

Younger members of the Dorset ACF *Ten Tors Challenge* team, who completed the 35-mile course: (left to right) J Natoli, K Knight, E Brown, J Sutcliffe and B Hole. One of them said: "The event was like nothing I have ever experienced before, especially the end, when all of the people were cheering for me and my team I felt absolutely incredible."

Cadets from Devon ACF on an Adventure Training exercise in the Los Pecos Mountains, Spain: standing (left to right) Laura Reddy, Daniel Giles, Laura Heeley, Nathan Moore, Rebecca Lockhead, Ben Bament, Joseph Southwick, WSI Julie Leake; kneeling (left to right) Greg Barnes, Tom Grant, Maj David Waterworth, Dale Munn-Tyrell, Lauren Tolley.

They were responsible for the protection of Camp Bastion and, on arrival in Afghanistan, there was new equipment to be mastered, including the .50 *Browning*, before the platoons rotated through various important tasks: guarding the main gate, manning the defensive 'sangars' and providing a quick reaction force. Although shooting incidents were not uncommon, the main gate sentries, Cpl Holloway and Pte Allen, were taken aback by the arrival of a bullet-riddled provisions truck. They were even more surprised when the Afghan driver emerged from his blood-soaked cab and hurriedly explained that, following an ambush on the road from Kandahar, he had managed to accelerate out of danger, before dropping his wounded passengers at the hospital and completing his delivery round at Camp Bastion.

Chapter 24

Catterick
(including Iraq 2006)
2004 – 2007

This final chapter follows the fortunes of the 1st Battalion, as well as covering developments within the wider Regimental family, as the independent existence of The Devonshire and Dorset Regiment drew to a close after forty-eight years of distinguished service. The 1st Battalion moved into Alma Barracks, Catterick in April 2004, becoming part of 12 Brigade, within 2 Division. The immediate operational requirement was to retrain in the mechanised infantry role while, from a Regimental angle, it was important to strengthen county ties after two years in Northern Ireland. While remaining on call for a return to the Province should the security situation deteriorate, the focus was on technical

On 4 May 2005 the Regiment exercised its right to march through Plymouth 'with bayonets fixed, drums beating and Colours flying': CSM Harvey keeps a watchful eye on his guard.

Over 1,000 members of the Regiment marched through Plymouth on Regimental Day, 4 May 2005: this shot of the 1st Battalion shows some of the vital preparatory work for such an important and high-profile occasion.

conversion courses: driving, signalling and gunnery. The Mortar Platoon had the particular challenge of mastering a new fire control system.

In mid-year the Regiment was well represented in the West Country. The Rifle Volunteers once again provided support to the *Ten Tors Challenge* while many of our cadets were amongst the 2,400 participants. On 29 May 2004 the Regimental family gathered for a memorable Regimental Day at Sherborne with a service in the Abbey, a freedom march through the town, a dinner and reception at Sherborne School and a reunion in the Digby Hall. A week later there were major commemorative events to celebrate the sixtieth anniversary of the Normandy landings: regular and TA soldiers and Old Comrades visited Normandy in strength as part of Ex *Janners' Landing*. Apart from the beaches themselves, there were also pilgrimages to Hill 112 and Arnhem, where 4 and 5 Dorset distinguished themselves. The 1st Battalion training cycle culminated in a fiercely-contested H Jones Competition, which took place in Kielder Forest and at Otterburn and was deservedly won by 8 Platoon.

In July 2004 the Government announced a spending review and an evaluation of the options that would lead to an appropriate Future Army Structure. At that stage few details were given, beyond the dispiriting news that four regular infantry battalions were to be amalgamated or disbanded. Understandable uncertainty over the Regiment's future could not be allowed to affect the focus on the job in hand as the British Army's commitments intensified. There were very few gaps in Lieutenant Colonel Toffer Beattie's diary when he took over command of the 1st Battalion from

Lieutenant Colonel Storrie in August 2004. That same month Support Company ran cadres on Salisbury Plain, members of the Recce Platoon attended the Combined Arms Tactical Trainer and the Battalion team won the 2 Division Biathlon Competition. That autumn the 1st Battalion took part in Ex *Janners' Launch* on Salisbury Plain: having commenced with company-level phases, it culminated in the first full test of the Battalion's mechanised infantry skills since its arrival at Catterick. As if this were not enough, the Battalion remained on call for duty in Northern Ireland and A Company briefly returned to Magilligan for public order validation. Since the start of the new millennium, overstretch in the British Army had resulted in the recruitment of a number of high-quality soldiers from Fiji. Those who joined the 1st Battalion swiftly made their mark, both by their invaluable contribution to the rugby team and also by their traditional and colourful celebrations on 10 October, Fiji's National Day.

In late November 2004 the Colonel of the Regiment was able to announce more detail on the future of the Regiment. It would be joining the Light Division and, in the interim, would become The Devonshire and Dorset Light Infantry. At the same time there were thoughts that all the Regiments of The Light Division might ultimately combine to form a new, large Regiment. That winter there were changes amongst key Regimental personnel in the counties as Lieutenant Colonel Leonard handed over to Lieutenant Colonel Charles Cooper as Curator of the Keep Military Museum and Lieutenant Colonel Squires retired as Assistant Regimental Secretary, to be replaced by Major Don Jellard, formerly RSM and QM of the 1st Battalion.

Naturally, changes revolving around the Future Army Structure were not allowed to divert attention from soldiering. The new year began with field-firing at Otterburn, range work at Pirbright and adventurous training at Leek in Staffordshire and Penhale

The Officers' and Warrant Officers' and Sergeants' Mess football teams pose after a match at Catterick in 2004, which the latter won by an impressive 6-1. They include, standing (left to right) WO2 Penhaligan, Capt Davies, Sgt Wadeson, Sgt Brown, Capt Donovan, Capt Skinner, Lt Ficke, Sgt Thomas, 2Lt Godfrey, Lt Allen, Sgt Weedon, CSgt Flower, Lt Steevenson, Sgt Trivett, Lt Owen, Sgt Lash; kneeling (left to right) Capt Larone, Sgt Jones, Lt Col Storrie, WO1 Griffiths, WO2 Campbell, Sgt Wyatt, WO2 Scarrott.

in Cornwall. Particular attention was paid to the requirements of specialist platoons as the Mortar Platoon worked closely with the Battalion's Close Support Light Battery during Ex *Tartan Blizzard* while the Anti-tank Platoon converted to *Javelin*, the 'fire-and-forget' missile that replaced *Milan*. The 1st Battalion spent the early months of 2005 preparing for Ex *Wessex Warrior*, that summer's test exercise on Salisbury Plain. The work-up included FIBUA training at Whinney Hill, field-firing at Warcop and the H Jones Competition, which was held on Dartmoor in May, and was won by the Recce Platoon.

On Salamanca Day, 22 July 2005, the Devon and Dorsets became the Devon and Dorset Light Infantry (DDLI). On moving from the Prince of Wales's Division to the Light Division, members of the Regiment adopted the Light Infantry green beret. It was also confirmed that, on 1 February 2007, we would amalgamate with the Royal Gloucester, Berkshire and Wiltshire Light Infantry (RGBWLI), thereby achieving the reduction of an infantry battalion in the British Army's order of battle. On 24 November 2005 The Queen formally approved the formation of The Rifles and the Charter was signed by the Colonels of all the forming regiments of the Light Division the following day. Reflecting our historical seniority, the combined DDLI/RGBWLI would become the 1st Battalion, The Rifles (1 Rifles), the senior battalion in a new seven-battalion regiment that included the Royal Green Jackets and the Light Infantry. The inevitable sadness at the end of an era was tempered by the exciting professional news that 1 DDLI would deploy to Iraq in April 2006 on Op *Telic 8*.

That autumn preparations began for the operational tour in Iraq. A wide range of specialist skills had to be learned and relevant courses included language, search and surveillance, photography and first aid. Ex *Alexander Kamal*, held that October, focused on staff procedures while 1 DDLI also provided enemy forces for Ex *Loyal Ledger*, the 19 Brigade test exercise. Following a two-week range package at Lydd, the Recce Group flew to Iraq in late February. The following month Ex *Desert Dragon*, which tested staff procedures, took place in Paderborn with 20 Armoured Brigade, under whose command the 1st Battalion would come in Basra. After a confirmatory exercise at Stanford, conducted by the Operational Training Advisory Group, deployment commenced on 16 April.

1st Battalion in Iraq 2006
On arrival in Iraq the 1st Battalion had a few days of acclimatisation and theatre-specific training at the Shaiba Logistics Base (SLB), before taking over from the 9/12 Lancers as the Basra Rural South Battle Group on 28 April. The four companies were dispersed: A Company was co-located with BG HQ at the SLB, with responsibility for Az Zubayr; B Company was based at the Palace in Basra, with responsibility for the Al Faw peninsula; C Company was at Um Qasr, Iraq's only deep water port, working closely with US forces in the border town of Safwan while 1 DDLI also provided the Brigade Surveillance Company (BSC), under the command of 20 Armoured Brigade at Basra

Air Station, which assumed responsibility for Op *Resilient* at Al Amarah.

In May Op *Tyne* was a Brigade 'surge', or show of force, into Basra to counter the increasingly adverse influence of rogue politicians and local militia, with the result that the Provincial Council re-engaged with British Forces for the first time since the previous September, when two British soldiers had had to be rescued from Jameat Police Station. Later the same month A Company was in the forefront of Op *Merrivale*, a search-and-arrest task that unearthed a cache of IED components. In July Op *Test* resulted in the arrest of Sajid Badr, a local militia leader, after several weeks of intelligence gathering. During the follow-up to this arrest Corporal John (George) Cosby, a team leader in the BSC, was killed in an aggressive fire fight. The same month the Maysan Battle Group was relocated as part of Op *Oyster*: three DDLI companies covered the move and Pte Attrill was extremely fortunate to escape serious injury when a bullet penetrated his helmet, passing round the inside, and leaving no

The CO's Rover Group with the Colours at the Memorial to the Missing 1914-21 in Basra, which commemorates British soldiers who were killed in Mesopotamia during the First World War – including Devons and Dorsets – and have no known grave: the group includes Capt Boswell, Capt Hale, Cpl O'Flanagan, Sgt Mockridge, Lt Col Beattie, Pte Whippy, Cpl Hines and Pte Nadredre.

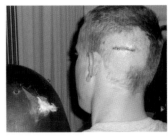

Capt White poses with a relaxed group of friendly Iraqis, Op *Telic*, 2006.

One close shave leads to another! For the benefit of the camera, Pte Attrill shows off just how lucky he was to escape serious injury when a bullet penetrated his helmet.

While serving in southern Iraq, the 1st Battalion had a large tactical area of responsibility, which was criss-crossed by waterways: high-speed 'rigid raiders' were frequently the most effective method of covering the area.

Forsaking the traditional *Land Rover*, Ptes Edwards, Baker and Royle pose in their preferred mode of transport, Op *Telic*, 2006: a John Deere *Gator* utility vehicle sporting Regimental colours.

Maj Wingfield, Capt Robertson and WO2 Chapman of C Coy work on the 'hearts and minds' of the younger members of the population of Basra.

Maj Murray, OC B Coy, halts his vehicle patrol in a wadi.

'Showing the flag': a *Land Rover* patrol in the Iraqi desert. Correct identification of vehicles from the air is of paramount importance in confused, operational contact situations.

The 1st Battalion provided the Brigade Surveillance Company, whose Team Commanders are seen in photograph below: (left to right) Cpl Eastwood, Sgt Neale, Cpl Keeley, Cpl Thompson, Sgt Mason, Cpl Jones, Cpl Wallace; kneeling (left to right) Sgt Bending, Cpl Cosby and Cpl Green. Cpl Cosby was killed in a clash with militants north of Basra on 16 Jul 2006.

Wearing the new range of body armour, a soldier from the 1st Battalion keeps an eye open for any signs of trouble on the open road, Iraq, 2006.

Bearing in mind the ever-present danger from IEDs (Improvised Explosive Devices), helicopters were frequently used in Iraq: a *Merlin* medium-lift helicopter takes off.

more than a small scar. In September B and C Companies were relieved by the theatre reserve battalion from Cyprus, enabling them to form part of 20 Armoured Brigade's 'surge' operations, Op *Salamanca* and later Op *Sinbad*, which continued through to the end of the tour. As part of Op *Brixham*, A Company provoked the insurgents into an unwise redeployment of their armoury, leading to the recovery of six weapons.

A covert search by the BSC, Op *Stingray*, led to the discovery of around 70 artillery and mortar shells (potential IEDs), which were destroyed in situ the following morning. During Op *Belstone* 2 Platoon were searching houses in Az Zubayr when they captured a key target, Ahmed Juboori, together with a fully-equipped, three-man rocket team. By contrast with these military tasks, 1 DDLI hosted a much-appreciated, 'hearts and minds' Ramadan dinner at the SLB for local tribal leaders and politicians

Although the writing says 'House for Sale', callsign 30A were making a wake-up call with a sledge hammer, Op *Toledo*, Az Zubayr.

on 19 October. The 1st Battalion's final operational task was Op *Citadel,* which led to the capture of Sameer Sangu, one of Basra Province's five 'Most Wanted', on 24 October. The strike group main body arrived simultaneously from three directions, with low loaders simulating a routine British Forces convoy, thus neutralising Sangu's experienced look-outs. On 12 November 2006 1 DDLI handed over to 1 Yorks: 2,500 members of the Regimental Family attended the homecoming parade at Catterick six days later.

Within weeks of returning from Iraq, the 1st Battalion started to reorganise itself in preparation for 1 February 2007, when it would form the core of 1 Rifles. Some months earlier all the officers, non-commissioned officers and soldiers had been asked to indicate which of the Rifles' regular battalions they wished to join. A key feature of the Future Army Structure was that those serving – and particularly their families – would be able to enjoy a more stable existence. To that end, as well as 1 Rifles' permanent station at Chepstow, conveniently close to the West Country, there were to be battalions of The Rifles stationed in Edinburgh, at Bulford, in Paderborn and at Ballykinler. The last three postings were already well known to many members of the 1st Battalion and that fact naturally influenced the decision that some took. In the event the 1st Battalion provided some 60% of the personnel for 1 Rifles, with most of the balance coming from 1 RGBWLI.

The final, emotional Regimental occasion took place on 27 January 2007, when the last stand of Colours of the 1st Battalion joined its two predecessors, and those of the 4th Battalion, in the Regimental Chapel in Exeter Cathedral. The entire Regimental Family was represented: there were guards from the 1st Battalion, from the Rifle Volunteers, and also from both Devon and Dorset Army Cadet Forces while the Old Comrades' Association mustered more than 1,000 members on parade. The Police said that they had never seen Exeter High Street so thronged with people as the Regiment marched past its Colonel-in-Chief 'with bayonets fixed, drums beating and

The sun sets on the 1st Battalion's final operational tour, Op *Telic*, Iraq, 2006.

The 1st Battalion.

The Rifle Volunteers.

The Regimental Family on Parade, 27 January 2007

The families.

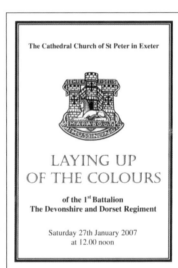

The Cathedral Church of St Peter in Exeter

LAYING UP
OF THE COLOURS

of the 1st Battalion
The Devonshire and Dorset Regiment

Saturday 27th January 2007
at 12.00 noon

The Cadets.

The Regimental Association.

On the saluting dais in front of the City's historic Guildhall: (left to right) Lt Gen Delves, the Lord Mayor of Exeter, the Duke of Kent, the Lord Lieutenant of Dorset and the Lord Lieutenant of Devon.

At St. George's Hall the Duke of Kent met a number of Regimental widows, including Mrs Sara Jones, Mrs Jenny Bond, Mrs Jean Tucker, Mrs Liz Biles, Mrs Joan Brown and Mrs Cynthia Walters.

The Cathedral Green was packed with those waiting to take their seats for the service.

The Colour Party approaches the doors of Exeter Cathedral between two files of the Old Comrades' Association, 27 Jan 2007: (on the left) Messrs Coombes, M Pike, A Pike, Riorden, Simpson, Gilbert and Northcot; (on the right) Messrs Old, Janes, Hendrick, Lloyd, Cook, Crawford, Cree, Perrin, Horn and Bennett.

At the reception in St. George's Hall, the Duke of Kent meets C/Sgts Thomas, Ratcliffe and Pinnell.

In Exeter Cathedral the address is given by the Right Rev John Kirkham, former Bishop of Sherborne and Bishop to the Forces.

The Drums give a final display for guests at the Regimental reception, 27 Jan 2007.

Colours flying'. After the formal service in the Cathedral, there was a Civic Reception hosted by the Regiment for friends and supporters. There was also the traditional Regimental Association gathering in St. George's Hall, with specially-brewed bottles of *Salamanca Ale* available in abundance. That evening there was a splendid dinner in honour of the Regiment, hosted by the Lord Mayor of Exeter, in the City's Guildhall.

Speaking from the pulpit in Exeter Cathedral, the Right Reverend John Kirkham, formerly Bishop of Sherborne and Bishop to the Forces, addressed the Regimental Family using these well-chosen words: "May you continue to be faithful; faithful in giving honour unto God; faithful in preserving the great traditions of the past, and taking them with you into the future; faithful in upholding Christian values; faithful in working for justice and peace. If you remain faithful to these things, what you have lived and fought for and many have suffered and died for will not have been in vain. The good tradition of this Regiment will live on and your future will be even greater than your past."

In St. George's Hall, at the end of a long day, Maj Gen Shortis formally thanks the Volunteer Band and Corps of Drums for their outstanding contribution to Regimental life over many years.

The Colours join the previous Colours of the 1st and 4th Battalions in the Regimental Chapel, where they will remain in perpetuity: Lt West (Queen's Colour), Lt Clayden (Regimental Colour); Escorts: WO2 Penhaligan, CSgt Dickson and CSgt Mockridge.

Roll of Honour

Members of The Devonshire and Dorset Regiment and The Rifle Volunteers

Died as a Result of Enemy Action

Pte C P Stentiford	1 D and D	21 Jan 1972	Northern Ireland
Sgt I M Harris	1 D and D	10 Feb 1972	Northern Ireland
Pte D M Champ	1 D and D att from WFR	10 Feb 1972	Northern Ireland
Cpl S A Windsor	1 D and D att to 1 DERR	6 Nov 1974	Northern Ireland
LCpl D A Dumbleton	1 D and D	2 Jun 1975	Cyprus
Lt Col H Jones VC OBE	2 PARA late D and D	28 May 1982	Falkland Islands
Cpl G T Jeffery	1 D and D	7 Apr 1983	Northern Ireland
LCpl S W Taverner	1 D and D	5 Nov 1983	Northern Ireland
Pte J P Kitulagoda	The Rifle Volunteers	28 Jan 2004	Afghanistan
Cpl J J Cosby	1 DDLI	6 Jul 2006	Iraq

Pte C P Stentiford

Sgt I M Harris

Pte D M Champ

Cpl S A Windsor

LCpl D A Dumbleton

Lt Col H Jones

Cpl G T Jeffery

LCpl S W Taverner

Pte J P Kitulagoda

Cpl J J Cosby

Died While Serving

LCpl R G Horlock	20 May 1959	Cyprus
Pte C J Gilbert	16 Dec 1961	England
WO2 K J Rooke	12 Dec 1963	England
Pte G A Hardy	22 Jan 1965	Northern Ireland
Pte P M Yorke	1 Jun 1966	England
Cpl Hadfield	15 Sep 1966	Germany
Lt Col C Chettle MC	16 Feb 1967	England
Col P T Willcocks MBE MC	18 May 1967	England
LCpl N R Joseph	24 Jul 1969	Germany
Cpl W J Benney	17 Dec 1970	Malta
Pte B Essex	24 Mar 1971	Malta
CSgt S C Sanders	6 Aug 1971	England
Cpl D O'Brien	19 Sep 1971	Malta
Cpl M G Elmes	23 Sep 1971	Malta
LCpl M L Phillips	10 Oct 1972	British Honduras
Cpl L Pearse	24 Feb 1973	England
Jnr Sldr A Pett	15 Nov 1975	Wales
Pte M J Blampey	10 Jul 1976	England
Pte M D Leaver	3 Sep 1977	Germany
Pte R J Turner	22 Jan 1978	Germany
Pte J Whelton	2 Mar 1978	Germany
Cpl R R Knott	15 Aug 1979	Wales
Pte G Major	24 Dec 1979	Germany
Sgt D G Penwill	30 Mar 1982	England
CSgt C A Hann	26 Oct 1983	England
CSgt C G Jeffery	7 May 1984	England
Cfn K A J Burrows	26 Nov 1985	Germany
Cfn T J Williams	25 Jul 1987	Wales
Pte S R Truan	16 Apr 1988	England
Col J J F Field OBE MC	18 Sep 1988	England
Cfn W Tomlinson	26 Mar 1989	England
WO2 (RQMS) F D Besien	24 May 1989	Northern Ireland
LCpl K P Dearlove	23 Jul 1989	Northern Ireland
Cpl P F Bolt	11 Jul 1991	England
Lt Col J W White OBE	23 Oct 1992	England
CSgt D J O'Rourke	17 May 1994	England
Col C J Biles OBE	2 Jun 1994	Scotland
Pte M A Smith	9 Jun 1994	Canada
Pte J S Willson	20 Jul 1994	Canada
Pte B J Matthews	31 Jan 1995	Germany
Pte V S Hole	23 Jun 1995	Bosnia
Pte W J Passmore	2 Jun 1997	England
Pte S J Evans	9 Aug 1998	England
Pte C I Berry	15 Sep 1998	England
LCpl W N Vanstone	6 Dec 1999	Bosnia
CSgt J W Newcombe	20 Dec 2001	England
LCpl L R Read	6 Dec 2002	Scotland
LCpl M T Hughes	7 Dec 2002	Scotland
Maj C R F Petchey	5 Sep 2004	France

'We Will Remember Them'

Regimental Honours and Awards

Honours and Awards are listed in order of precedence and then by date

| VC | GCB | KBE | CB | CMG | CVO | CBE | DSO |

Victoria Cross (posthumous) (VC)
Lt Col H Jones OBE PARA, 11 Oct 1982

Knight Grand Cross of the Order of the Bath (GCB)
Gen Sir John Wilsey KCB CBE, 30 Dec 1995

Knight Commander of the Order of the Bath (KCB)
Lt Gen A J Archer OBE, 12 Jun 1976
Lt Gen J F W Wilsey CBE, 31 Dec 1990

Knight Commander of the Order of St Michael and St George (KCMG)
Maj Gen W H A Bishop CB CMG CVO OBE, 13 Jun 1964

Knight Commander of the Order of the British Empire (KBE)
Lt Gen C N G Delves CBE DSO, 14 Jun 2003

Companion of the Order of the Bath (CB)
Maj Gen H A Borradaile DSO, 13 Jun 1959
Brig P Gleadell CBE DSO, 14 Jul 1959
Maj Gen A S Jeapes OBE MC, 13 Jun 1987
Maj Gen C T Shortis CBE, 11 Jun 1988
Maj Gen B H Dutton CBE, 14 Jun 1997

Companion of the Order of St Michael and St George (CMG)
Maj Gen W H A Bishop CB OBE, 31 Dec 1960

Commander of the Royal Victorian Order (CVO)
Maj Gen W H A Bishop CB CMG OBE, 3 Mar 1961
Lt Col V A J Heald DSO MBE MC, 11 Jun 1966

Commander of the Order of the British Empire (CBE)

Col J L Jones, 1 Jan 1959
Brig P H Brind DSO OBE, 1 Jan 1962
Brig C T Shortis OBE, 21 Oct 1980
Col J F W Wilsey, 16 Apr 1985
Brig B H Dutton OBE, 15 May 1990

Col D C N Shaw MBE, 31 Dec 1992
Col S D Young OBE, 10 May 1996
Maj Gen C N G Delves DSO OBE, 31 Dec 1996
Col T W Hambrook OBE, 5 Dec 1997
Col R H D Toomey MBE, 12 Jun 2004

Companion of the Distinguished Service Order (DSO)
Maj C N G Delves, 11 Oct 1982

Lieutenant of the Royal Victoria Order (LVO)
Lt Col R Jury, 26 Feb 1979

OBE

Officer of the Order of the British Empire (OBE)

Lt Col C F King, 1 Jan 1959
Lt Col Q D T Hogg, 1 Jan 1959
Lt Col O G W White DSO, 13 Jun 1959
Col The Lord Clifford, 1 Jan 1961
Lt Col D E Harris, 2 Jun 1962
Maj C C Metcalfe MC, 1 Jan 1964
Lt Col A J Archer MBE, 1 Jan 1965
Lt Col J P Randle MC, 12 Jun 1965
Lt Col P Burdick, 24 Sept 1974
Lt Col D B Edwards, 16 May 1975
Lt Col A S Jeapes MC, 11 Jun 1977
Lt Col C T Shortis MBE, 13 Dec 1977
Col C W G Bullocke, 8 Jan 1980
Col M F R Bullock, 14 Jun 1980
Lt Col H Jones MBE, 31 Dec 1980
Lt Col J M Hewitt, 16 Jun 1981
Lt Col J F W Wilsey, 31 Dec 1982
Col F J Pike, 16 Jun 1984

Lt Col J J F Field MC, 16 Jun 1984
Lt Col M D Embury MBE, 16 Jun 1984
Maj B H Dutton MBE, 16 Jun 1984
Lt Col H G L Playfair, 31 Dec 1988
Col P D Baldry TD, 17 Jun 1989
Lt Col C N G Delves DSO, 16 Jun 1990
Lt Col C T Rogers. 26 Sept 1991
Lt Col C J Biles MBE, 13 Jun 1992
Lt Col J W White, 27 Oct 1992
Lt Col M F Forey, 31 Dec 1992
Lt Col A B S Collings MBE, 31 Dec 1993
Lt Col T W Hambrook MBE, 22 Nov 1994
Lt Col S D Young MBE, 22 Nov 1994
Lt Col J R Cook MBE MC, 14 Nov 1995
Lt Col A J S Storrie, 19 Apr 2002
Lt Col M F Richardson, 31 Oct 2003
Lt Col A W Thornburn MBE, 31 Dec 2003

MBE

Member of the Order of the British Empire (MBE)

Maj G G Baker, 13 Jun 1959
Maj A J Archer, 1 Jan 1960
WO1 B M V Staddon, 11 Jun 1960
Maj G W Blake, 8 Jun 1963
Maj S I Fulford TD, 1 Jan 1964
Maj M J C H Saunders, 13 Jun 1964
Maj A D Rouse, 1 Jan 1965
Maj M D Embury, 1 Jan 1965
Maj D P Lovejoy, 12 Jun 1965
Maj J E K Goodbody, 12 Jun 1965
Maj C T Shortis, 1 Jan 1975
Maj J Freer-Smith, 14 Jun 1975
Maj R S Pollard, 12 Jun 1976
Maj R V Woodiwiss, 11 Jun 1977
Maj H Jones, 13 Dec 1977
Maj B H Dutton, 3 Jun 1978
Capt D C N Shaw, 19 Sept 1978
Maj M P Nott, 16 Jun 1979
Maj G B Blight, 14 Jun 1980
Maj A B S Collings, 15 Jun 1982
Capt A P Solway, 31 Dec 1982
Capt L D Brown, 31 Dec 1983
Maj A W Thornburn, 17 Apr 1984
Capt R W Barnes, 16 Apr 1985
Maj W C Walter, 15 Apr 1986

Maj C J Biles, 14 Apr 1987
Maj T W Hambrook, 13 Oct 1987
Capt P D Stacey, 12 Apr 1988
Maj S D Young, 16 May 1989
Capt H Jellard, 15 May 1990
Maj D M M Steevenson, 15 Jun 1991
Maj J N Speakman, 31 Dec 1992
Capt G D McMeeken, 31 Dec 1992
Maj C L Pape, 31 Dec 1993
Maj M J Henderson, 31 Dec 1994
Maj M P King, 31 Dec 1994
Maj A J S Storrie, 14 Nov 1995
Maj J F Watson, 10 May 1996
Maj R H D Toomey, 10 May 1996
WO2 L J Braddon, 10 May 1996
Maj W M Sharpe, 14 Jun 1997
Maj T J J Saunders, 12 Jun 1999
Maj R T H Jones, 16 Jun 2001
WO2 V S Williams, 15 Jun 2002
Sgt R J Rutherford, 31 Dec 2002
Maj M J Edkins, 30 Sept 2003
WO2 A Holcombe, 31 Dec 2003
Maj R C Steptoe, 12 Jun 2004
Maj P S Messervy, 11 Jun 2005

Military Cross (MC)
Lt A S Jeapes, 25 Aug 1959
Capt J J F Field, 3 Oct 1972
Cpl S J G Harvey, 10 May 1996
LCpl N A T Coleman, 15 Dec 2006

Queen's Gallantry Medal (QGM)
Sgt G F Riley, 24 Sep 1974
CSgt P C Jones, 15 Apr 1980
Pte J P Richards, 17 Apr 1984

British Empire Medal (BEM)
CSgt D R Roberts, 10 Jun 1964
D/Maj R Norsworthy, 1 Jan 1965
Cpl B Colley, 12 Jun 1965
Sgt L T Thorne, 1 Jan 1966
CSgt J Mitchell, 31 Dec 1975
Cpl A G Swanson, 1 Jul 1980
CSgt D E Newitt, 1 Jan 1981

George Medal (GM)
WO2 P C Jones, 16 Oct 1984

Military Medal (MM)
Sgt R E Bennett, 9 Apr 1974

Cpl C C Gillespie, 31 Oct 1989

Bar to QGM
Sgt C C Gillespie, 10 May 1996

WO2 G A E Spiller, 13 Jun 1982
WO2 P Barrett, 21 Dec 1982
Sgt A R Olde, 31 Dec 1982
D/Maj A H Cox, 31 Dec 1983
SSgt P W M Williams, 16 Oct 1984
Sgt A J Triggs, 31 Dec 1987
CSgt G R Ashton, 30 Dec 1989

MC

GM

Queen's Commendation for Valuable Service (QCVS)
Maj I P Blewett, 22 Nov 1994
Maj M J Henderson, 22 Nov 1994
Capt D F H Jones, 22 Nov 1994
Pte C W Hill, 22 Nov 1994
Maj C J Biles, 9 May 1995
Lt Col J R Cook OBE MC, 10 May 1996
Maj M J Edkins, 10 May 1996

Capt M C J Lloyd, 10 May 1996
Maj Gen C N G Delves DSO OBE, 7 May 1999
Lt Col R H D Toomey MBE, 30 Oct 2001
Capt J C Pettitt, 23 Apr 2002
Lt Col A J S Storrie, 29 Apr 2003
Capt W J P Kelsall, 7 Sept 2004
Cpl D C Thomas, 7 Sept 2004

MM

Mention in Despatches
Capt D P Lovejoy, 14 Jul 1959
Cpl W C Walter, 14 Jul 1959
Maj R V Woodiwiss, 14 Dec 1965
2Lt N Marden, 3 Oct 1972
Cpl R F Bridgeman, 3 Oct 1972
Lt J W White, 24 Sept 1974
2Lt T W Hambrook, 8 Oct 1974
Maj J F W Wilsey, 13 Dec 1977
CSgt P MacPherson, 13 Dec 1977
Maj J J Reid, 13 Dec 1977
LCpl D R Taylor, 6 Jun 1978
Maj B H Dutton MBE, 8 Nov 1979
Capt C N G Delves, 8 Jan 1980
Maj C N G Delves, 15 Dec 1981
Lt Col J F W Wilsey, 15 Jun 1982
Maj G Jefferies, 15 Jun 1982
Capt L C Burrlock, 15 Jun 1982
WO2 A J Thompson, 15 Jun 1982

Cpl B S Hutt, 15 Jun 1982
Capt L D Brown, 14 Aug 1982
Sgt A G Swanson BEM, 12 Apr 1983
Lt Col P D King-Fretts, 16 Apr 1985
RSM H Jellard, 16 Apr 1985
WO2 T J Jackson, 15 Apr 1986
Cpl I S G Squires, 15 Apr 1986
LCpl L J Burton, 15 Apr 1986
Lt Col J J F Field OBE MC, 11 Nov 1986
Col D C N Shaw, 15 May 1990
Maj J D Gaye, 15 May 1990
Maj T W Hambrook MBE, 15 May 1990
Lt G S Snell, 15 May 1990
Maj D J M Ferguson RAMC, 29 Jun 1991
Maj I P Blewett, 12 May 1992
Pte A C Hawke, 22 Nov 1994
CSgt A M Donovan, 10 May 1996
CSgt E C Dean, 18 Mar 2005
Sgt P Poole-Reeves, 10 May 2006

QGM

BEM

Queen's Commendation for Bravery (QCB)
LCpl V K Turner, 9 Feb 1960
LCpl C M Burt, 3 Nov 2000
Sgt D M Budden, 6 Sept 2004
LCpl D A Jones, 7 Sept 2004

Meritorious Service Medal (MSM)
WO2 C J R Walters
QMSI E G Baker
RSM L J Webber
WO2 D Gilbert

Army Emergency Reserve Decoration (ERD)
Lt (Hon Maj) R E L Wingate

ERD and Clasp
Maj H J Hickling

Non Gazetted Awards
Queen's Commendation
Sgt D J Knight

Joint Commander's Commendation
Sgt A J Day
LCpl L M Scott
Maj N R Holmes
Pte C J Rolf
Sgt O P Vernon

GOC's Commendation
Sgt W M Kinson
Lt T W House
Sgt M Braddon
CSgt M Braddon
Capt H E Allen
Cpl A Foster
LCpl M Griffiths
Pte A S Davey
Pte N E Ewings
Cpl C I Campbell
LCpl R J Gaskell
LCpl M P P Mockridge
Cpl G J Perkins
CSgt D Turley
WO2 M J Henderson
LCpl B Gilley
Sgt A L McColl
Cpl S Sims

Queen's Commendation for Brave Conduct (QCBC)
Pte P E J Bounden, 9 Aug 1983

Efficiency Decoration (Territorial) (TD)
Capt M C Fausset
Maj J C Lillies
Maj M S O'F Cook MBE
Lt (Hon Capt) J N Davey
Maj J N Speakman
Capt I R Upshall
Maj J G Harrison
Maj A N Roberts
Maj I T Mereweather

C-in-C's Commendation
Revd R Clayton-Jones
Capt M H Jarrett

C-in-C's Certificate
S T Avery

Sgt G S Titley
LCpl A P Smith
WO2 P A Connor
Cpl G A Parmenter
LCpl T E Dempsey
LCpl S W Taverner
CSgt K J Finnamore
Cpl R J Read
LCpl K D Jesty
LCpl K F Squires
Pte M V Lewis
CSgt A K Penhaligan
Pte R P Goss
Cpl D Gough
Sgt M A Borlace
Capt G J Colton
Sgt K J Potter
Sgt K D Pinnell

Regimental Appointments

1st Battalion

Commanding Officer

Lt Col G R Young OBE, May 58 – Nov 58
Lt Col R H Wheatley DSO, Nov 58 – Nov 60
Lt Col P T Willcocks MBE MC, Nov 60 – Oct 62
Lt Col J P Randle MC, Oct 62 – Apr 65
Lt Col A J Archer OBE, Apr 65 – Sep 67
Lt Col A D Rouse MBE, Sep 67 – Oct 69
Lt Col D P Lovejoy MBE, Oct 69 – Mar 72
Lt Col P Burdick, Mar 72 – Sep 74
Lt Col C T Shortis MBE, Sep 74 – Jun 77
Lt Col C W G Bullocke, Jun 77 – Dec 79
Lt Col J F W Wilsey, Dec 79 – Jun 82

Lt Col P D King-Fretts, Jun 82 – Oct 84
Lt Col B H Dutton OBE, Oct 84 – Feb 87
Lt Col D C N Shaw MBE, Feb 87 – Sep 87
Lt Col C J Biles MBE, Sep 89 – Mar 92
Lt Col S D Young MBE, Mar 92 – Feb 95
Lt Col J R Cook MBE MC, Feb 95 – Sep 97
Lt Col J F Watson MBE, Sep 97 – Mar 00
Lt Col R H D Toomey MBE, Mar 00 – Jun 02
Lt Col A J S Storrie OBE, Jun 02 – Aug 04
Lt Col C J Beattie, Aug 04 – Jan 07

Second-in-Command

Maj D A Gilchrist, May 58 – Aug 60
Maj J S G Walenn MBE MC, Aug 60 – May 61
Maj C Chettle MC, May 61 – Aug 62
Maj J D Freer-Smith, Aug 62 – Jun 64
Maj M F R Bullock, Jun 64 – Jun 65
Maj M J Reynolds, Jun 65 – Oct 67
Maj R J Martin MC Glosters, Oct 67 – Jun 68
Maj P Burdick, Jun 68 – Jun 70
Maj G B Blight, Jun 70 – Jun 71
Maj D B Edwards, Jun 71 – Oct 72
Maj C W G Bullocke, Oct 72 – Dec 75
Maj J T Wilson WFR, Dec 75 – Dec 76
Maj J M Martin R Hamps, Dec 76 – Dec 78
Maj D G Thomas, Dec 78 – Jan 81
Maj J J Reid, Jan 81 – Feb 83

Maj R P Steptoe, Feb 83 – Jul 85
Maj J G T Dewar R Hamps, Jul 85 – Jun 87
Maj T W Hambrook, Jun 87 – Aug 88
Maj S D Young, Aug 88 – May 90
Maj G S Nicholls, May 90 – Dec 92
Maj J R Cook MBE MC, Dec 92 – Dec 93
Maj A J Trevis, Dec 93 – Dec 94
Maj D J Harrison, Dec 94 – Jan 97
Maj A W Field WFR, Jan 97 – Jul 98
Maj M J Edkins, Jul 98 – Jul 00
Maj D C E Field, Jul 00 – Mar 02
Maj T W House, Mar 02 – Oct 03
Maj N J Fenton QDG, Oct 03 – Sep 04
Maj A J Gales, Sep 04 – Jan 07

Adjutant

Capt E C Stones, May 58 – Oct 58
Capt B J Sims, Oct 58 – Dec 59
Capt D P Lovejoy, Dec 59 – Sep 60
Capt J W Tong, Sep 60 – May 62
Capt A G Laurie-Chiswell, May 62 – Jul 64
Capt C R M Green, Jul 64 – Feb 66
Capt N C Thompson Glosters, Feb 66 – Aug 66
Capt J Cobb, Aug 66 – Aug 68
Capt H Jones, Aug 68 – Jun 70
Capt J J F Field MC, Jun 70 – Jun 72
Capt B H Dutton, Jun 72 – Dec 73
Capt D R Roberts BEM, Dec 73 – Dec 74
Capt D C N Shaw, Dec 74 – Dec 75
Capt J D Forde R Hamps, Dec 75 – May 76
Capt J W White, May 76 – Sep 77
Capt S D Young, Sep 77 – May 79
Capt C J Biles, May 79 – May 81

Capt J D Gaye, May 81 – Oct 82
Capt G S Nicholls, Oct 82 – Dec 83
Capt D J Harrison, Dec 83 – Dec 85
Capt T J C Clayden, Dec 85 – Dec 87
Capt R W Barnes MBE, Dec 87 – Dec 89
Capt R H D Toomey, Dec 89 – Dec 90
Capt D C E Field, Dec 90 – Jul 92
Capt T W House, Jul 92 – Feb 94
Capt R A D Gibb, Feb 94 – Aug 95
Capt S M Weber, Aug 95 – Nov 97
Capt R T H Jones, Nov 97 – Sep 98
Capt M Fairhurst, Sep 98 – Apr 99
Capt A K G Millsop, Apr 99 – Sep 00
Capt J E F Bryant, Sep 00 – Jun 02
Capt M L Maynard, Jun 02 – Feb 04
Capt S M Davies, Feb 04 – Jul 05
Capt C W Boswell, Jul 05 – Jan 07

Regimental Sergeant Major

WO1 A T Coombe, May 58 – Jun 59
WO1 R S Pollard, Jun 59 – May 63
WO1 M P Nott, May 63 – Feb 64
WO1 A E Tizzard, May 64 – Jan 65
WO1 W Lucas, Mar 65 – Mar 68
WO1 P E Turney, Mar 68 – Dec 70
WO1 R H Simpson, Dec 70 – Jun 71
WO1 W Thacker, Jun 71 – May 74
WO1 L D Brown, May 74 – Dec 76
WO1 L C Burrlock, Dec 76 – Nov 79
WO1 J Wilding, Nov 79 – Dec 81
WO1 H Jellard, Dec 81 – Sep 83

WO1 M J Henderson, Sep 83 – Apr 85
WO1 P MacPherson, Apr 85 – Jan 88
WO1 G S Titley, Jan 88 – Jul 91
WO1 R J Cleverley, Jul 91 – Dec 93
WO1 K J Fitzgerald, Dec 93 – Jun 96
WO1 K J Finnamore, Jun 96 – Jun 98
WO1 J E Anning, Jun 98 – Apr 00
WO1 C B Smith, Apr 00 – Feb 02
WO1 M A Skinner, Feb 02 – Mar 04
WO1 M Griffiths, Apr 04 – Dec 05
WO1 M Hale, Jan 06 – Feb 06
WO1 R J Hunt, Mar 06 – Jan 07

Quartermaster

Maj H A S Titterington MBE, 1958 – 1961
Maj G W R Blake MBE, 1961 – 1963
Lt W C Harris, 1963 – 1964
Capt K Marquis, 1964 – 1967
Capt T Coombe, 1967 – 1968
Capt G E Street R Hamps, 1968 – 1971
Capt M P Nott, 1971 – 1973
Maj T Price RRW, 1973 – 1977
Capt D R Roberts BEM, 1977 – 1980
Capt T F Allen WFR, 1980 – 1982
Capt W Walter, 1982 – 1985

Maj L D Brown MBE, 1985 – 1987
Capt J Mitchell BEM, 1987 – 1989
Maj W G Evans Glosters, 1989 – 1991
Maj H Jellard MBE, 1991 – 1993
Maj M J Henderson, 1993 – 1996
Maj P R Mehrlich, 1996 – 2000
Capt R J Cleverley, 2000 – 2002
Capt W J P Kelsall, 2002 – 2004
Capt K J Finnamore, 2004 – 2006
Capt C B Smith, 2006 – 2007

4th Battalion
Commanding Officer

Lt Col R P Steptoe, 1987 – 1989
Lt Col C E Cooper, 1989 – 1992
Lt Col A W Thornburn MBE, 1992 – 1995

Lt Col A J B Edwards, 1995 – 1997
Lt Col M C Fausset TD, 1997 – 1999

Regimental Sergeant Major

WO1 C J Madders, 1987 – 1989
WO1 P W M Williams BEM, 1989 – 1992
WO1 W D Young, 1992 – 1993

WO1 A G Mace, 1993 – 1995
WO1 W J P Kelsall, 1995 – 1997
WO1 G Parmenter, 1997 – 1999

Rifle Volunteers
Commanding Officer

Lt Col D J Harrison, 1999 – 2001
Lt Col I P Blewett, 2001 – 2004

Lt Col J W Hall MBE LI, 2004 – 2006
Lt Col I T Mereweather, 2006 – 2007

The Colonel of the Regiment

ince 1958 there have been nine Colonels of The Devonshire and Dorset Regiment. This is an appointment like no other since, subject only to the formal approval of HM The Queen, it is in the Regiment's own gift. It is a thus a singular honour to be chosen as the Regiment's titular head, entrusted with nurturing and representing the Regiment's best interests. The Colonel of the Regiment, initially appointed for a period of five years, which may exceptionally be extended, stands apart from the chain of command. He is answerable only to the needs of the Regimental family in its widest sense. In the case of a County Regiment like the Devon and Dorsets, that entails considerable involvement in the affairs and needs of the two Counties, from which they derive their name, their soldiers and their ethos. The Colonel of the Regiment also keeps the Colonel-in-Chief abreast of Regimental developments.

Major-General
G N Wood,
CB CBE DSO MC
17 May 1958 –
25 February 1962

Internally, the Colonel of the Regiment's role is vital. Ably assisted by Regimental Headquarters, he is responsible for the recruitment and selection of potential officers, the Regiment's seed-corn. He also assists in the selection of future commanding officers from among those qualified for promotion and selected for possible appointment. At any one time

Major-General
H A Borradaile,
CB DSO
26 February 1962 –
6 February 1967

Brigadier
A E C Bredin,
DSO MC DL
7 February 1967 –
6 February 1977

General
Sir John Archer,
KCB OBE
7 February 1977 –
30 November 1979

Colonel
M F R Bullock,
OBE DL
1 December 1979 –
30 November 1984

Major-General
C T Shortis,
CB CBE
1 December 1984 –
31 May 1990

General
Sir John Wilsey,
GCB CBE DL
1 June 1990 –
31 December 1997

Major-General
B H Dutton,
CB CBE
1 January 1998 –
30 December 2002

the Regiment needs to groom for possible command at least seven officers of various ranks, ages and stages of career progression. The Colonel of the Regiment monitors the progress of these officers, in order to ensure the widest possible choice when the final decisions are taken. In this context, it is noteworthy that the Regiment has never had to import a commanding officer and has exported some six to other regiments. Indeed, the Colonels of the Regiment themselves have always been 'home-grown'.

As Chairman of the Trustees of the Regiment's various funds, assets, chapels, museums and property, the Colonel of the Regiment has onerous responsibilities for the history and traditions of the Regiment and the well-being of all members past and present, including former Devons and former Dorsets. For example, in the lengthy and complex negotiations that preceded the formation of The Rifles, the Colonel of the Regiment played a key role in representing the interests of The Regiment.

In conclusion the Colonel of the Regimental can best be described as the head of the family: chosen by the Regiment, for the Regiment.

Lieutenant-General Sir
Cedric Delves, KBE DSO
31 December 2002 –
31 January 2007

Freedom Cities, Boroughs and Towns

*S*hown below are the fifteen Cities, Boroughs and Towns which have granted their Freedom to the Regiment. The Freedom allows a Regiment to march through the streets 'with drums beating, bayonets fixed and Colours flying'. It is a special privilege and great honour to be given this Freedom, as it is a recognition of our close connections with our home counties and the esteem each has for the other.

Town of Lyme Regis	16 Aug 1945
Borough of Barnstaple	29 Jul 1946
Borough of Poole	11 Sept 1946
Town of Dorchester	12 Sept 1946
Town of Blandford Forum	18 Nov 1955
City of Exeter	11 May 1962
Borough of Bridport	12 Feb 1967
County Borough of Torbay	8 May 1973
Borough of Weymouth and Melcombe Regis	12 May 1973
Borough of Christchurch	9 Jul 1980
City of Plymouth	19 Mar 1988
Town of Sherborne	28 May 1994
Town of Gillingham	3 Oct 1998
Town of Shaftesbury	15 Apr 2000
Town of Exmouth	1 Jun 2002

Two representative
Freedom Scrolls.

Two more Freedom Scrolls.

SEMPER FIDELIS
MARABOUT
PRIMUS IN INDIS

THE C

Barnstaple

Exeter

Devon

Torbay

Plymouth

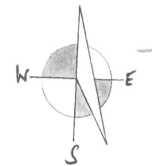

W —— E
S